WRITING WAR

A Guide to Telling Your Own Story

BY
Ron Capps

ISBN:146643502X
ISBN-13:978-1466435025

TO ABSENT FRIENDS

CONTENTS

Ron Capps

The generation that carried on the war has been set apart by its experience. To our great good fortune, in our youth our hearts were touched with fire. It was given to us to learn that life is a profound and passionate thing. While we are permitted to scorn nothing but indifference, we have seen with our own eyes, and it is for us to bear the report to those who come after us.

Oliver Wendell Holmes

from his memorial Day Address, 1884.

Ron Capps

ACKNOWLEDGMENTS

I wrote this book to serve as the core curriculum for the Veterans Writing Project, a 501(c)(3) non-profit based in Washington DC. The VWP provides no-cost writing seminars and workshops for veterans, active and reserve service members, and military family members.

Bill Black provided me with a great deal of sage advice in the creation of this book. His influence and insights are evident throughout. Any mistakes or shortfalls are mine alone. I should also point out where others' work is evident. The description of plot types in Chapter 6 are drawn from ideas Tim Wendel shared. The four stages of revision in Chapter 11 are the work of Mark Farrington. My friend Paul Barbagallo edited the manuscript, and many participants in our seminars have commented on the text as well. Thanks as well to Kate Trueblood for helping me find examples of writing by women veterans.

Neither this book nor the VWP would exist without the support of my friends and family. Thank you all.

WWW.VETERANSWRITING.ORG

WWW.O-DARK-THIRTY.ORG

WHY DO WE WRITE?

Only, I felt, by some such attempt to write history in terms of personal life could I rescue something that might be of value, some element of truth and hope and usefulness, from the smashing up of my own youth by the war.

Vera Brittain,
Testament of Youth

Before the written word existed, people passed information among themselves through spoken word, song, drumbeats or even handfuls of sticks or shells. Speech is a wonderful form of communication. It is powerful and, because it is delivered face to face (or at least it was before the invention of the telephone), it carries with it the additional meanings possible through gesture, intonation, posture, a wink and a nod, and so on. Nonetheless, it is impermanent. Once spoken and once heard, speech ceases to exist except in memory. It can be passed on but, as we know, information becomes distorted through repeated tellings.

So, in a way, we write to make our voices eternal, to give a sense of permanence to our ideas. In doing this, we presume that our ideas deserve permanence. We write because we believe at some level that we have something worth saying, worth saving.

We believe that we have some commentary on the human condition that is of value and should be remembered. We are very full of ourselves, aren't we?

French novelist (and paratrooper) Georges Perec said that we write because we have lived, nothing more. I think it might be a little different for each of us. Some of us write because we need to figure things out and writing is one way of doing that. Putting the words down on paper helps us think through an event or a story and come to a better understanding of it. Sometimes we do this simply because we need to get the story out, to tell it and be done with it. Writing turns the ideas into something concrete, something physical that we can then push away from ourselves. It can give us distance. Sometimes we write to express things that can't be said out loud. We may have some sense or experience that can't be expressed directly. Writing allows us to create metaphors, one thing that substitutes for or represents another, and gives us the chance to express something unexplainable.

So we write. We ponder and ruminate and then scribble and scratch or hunt and peck our way through a story. We write to tell a story. Some of us tell our stories easily. Some of us struggle to get the words onto the page; we anguish over every turn of phrase, over every plot choice. Joseph Heller said, "Every writer I know has trouble writing." Heller flew 60 combat missions as a bombardier in a B-25 on the Italian front during World War II. Compared to that, writing should be easy.

If you're reading this, it's safe to assume you want to become a better writer. Some people, allegedly even those who created the great-granddaddy of all graduate writing programs, the Writers' Workshop at the University of Iowa, believe that writing cannot be taught. That we are working together is a testament to our shared belief that even if it can't be taught, it can be learned. Together, we will find ways to learn.

It doesn't matter if you want to create a great work of literature or just put together your personal history to leave for your grandkids. This book can help you. At times it might seem that we're writing for someone else, but that's because we have to address lots of topics to make sure we can help both groups. I'm asking you now to tough it out. Stick with us. No matter what you want to write, you're nearly certain to come through this a better writer. So let's go.

*

Throughout the book we will read what others have written. We won't read for enjoyment. Don't get me wrong, it's fine if you enjoy what we read. But that's not the purpose. We read so we can learn how other writers put together their work. We ask, "what about this story is working well, and what isn't?"

When we talk about reading in this context, we should be clear that we're not talking about reading the way we look through the morning sports page: a quick check of the box scores, were there any major trades, how many strikeouts for the new reliever, any home runs for the aging slugger?

No, we're talking about giving something a close read in order to learn how the author has put together the work. What words does the author use? How are the sentences structured? Where is there tension? How does the author get the protagonist to overcome obstacles? What's the tone of the piece? What's the point of the story and what's its purpose—these are different.

We'll also write, of course. We'll write sentences and paragraphs and chapters and stories. We'll read each others' work and we will gently share with our colleagues what works for us and what doesn't. Then we'll revise. James Michener, a World War II Navy veteran, said of himself, "I'm not a good writer, but I'm an excellent re-writer."

We will ask of ourselves to be good writers and we will try to produce works of literary merit. This is a very high standard. Literature isn't a weather report (news) or a movie review (criticism), a political dissertation (academic) or a set of instructions (technical writing). Literary writing has an artistic purpose: It provides an aesthetic sensation to the reader. We may not always succeed in this, but we need to set goals. This is one of those points where some of you might get turned off. I can hear some of you saying "literary merit? I just want help organizing my personal history." Remember, this is a book for many different types of writers—you included. So stick with me. We're going to cover lots of ground.

John Cheever described good prose as "where one hears the rain [and] the noise of battle." I think what he is saying is that good prose engages the reader fully. It brings the reader completely into the scene, where one's mind imagines the sounds and tastes and smells of the moment. Cheever was a soldier in the Second World War. It is possible that writing saved his life. He was an infantryman scheduled to go ashore on D-Day, but was plucked from the ranks by an officer who read his first book and put him to work writing Army propaganda movies. Most of his infantry company was killed on the beaches of Normandy.

By now you will have noticed that the quotes we use as examples are from writers who are also veterans. There is a reason we do this. It is simply to impart the idea to you that others who have come before you from the ranks have succeeded in this endeavor; that it is possible.

Throughout this course, every passage we quote will be an example written by a veteran. Some served long ago: Guy du Maupassant was a soldier in the Franco-Prussian wars; Vera Brittain served as a nurse in WWI. Some served more recently: Kelly Kennedy was a soldier in the Gulf War and Somalia.

Four Quick Points.

It's on you.

Some of you have come to this program because you have something you really need to say. Maybe it's been inside you for a while now and sometimes you feel like if you don't say it you'll burst. We can help you. But remember, this is a writing program. We're here to learn about the craft of writing. Some of us who developed this program, well at least one of us, came home from the war in Afghanistan and struggled to re-enter civilian society. Writing helped. There is a handwritten poster on the walls of the office where we created this book that says, "either you control the story or the story controls you." We're going to learn about story telling in this book.

Maybe telling your story can help you control it. But here's the rub. If you need help, go get it. No one can get it for you. This is something you have to do for yourself. So saddle up and move out. We'll be here when you're ready.

On Grammar.

You'll find that there is no chapter in the book on grammar or punctuation. There are plenty of good grammar books out there and it's not our purpose here to supplant them. Go get one and make it your friend.

Browse the grammar handbooks at the library reference section or the bookstore. Look at the way the authors organize and present the material. Find one that you like, get a copy and use it. Look things up in the handbook regularly, even things you think you know. Actually one of the best ways to choose a handbook is to look up something you're confident of and see if you like the way the authors present it.

Most writers have their favorite, their go-to reference when something tricky comes up. I use the Random House *Webster's Grammar, Usage and Punctuation*. Some people swear by the *Little Brown Handbook*, others believe that Strunk & White's *The Elements of Style* is all you'll ever need. Journalists use one of numerous style guides, often the AP or New York *Times* manuals. Publishers often prefer the Chicago Manual of Style.

Remember that grammar and punctuation are tools. If you use them well, no one will notice; if you goof up, everyone will.

Forms and Facts.

The three principal forms of writing presented in this book are fiction, non-fiction, and poetry. It might not sound like much, but you can cover a lot of ground under these three. We won't get into playwriting or screenwriting, nor will we venture into blogging, journalism, technical, or academic writing. Eventually, writers find their place, whether it is as a journalist, essayist, or novelist, or maybe writing movies, memoirs or short stories.

We will spend loads of time on fiction and poetry as we move forward. But on non-fiction, we are obliged to quickly and directly address one particular issue: that of truth. When we write non-fiction, we make a contract with the reader (and with our editor and our publisher and all of their lawyers) that what we write is true. Not mostly true or pretty much the way things happened, except that we left out the stuff that didn't make us look good. The truth.

William Faulkner once said, "facts and truth really don't have much to do with each other." He might be right in a literary sense, but Faulkner was a novelist, a fiction writer. He was also a prodigious liar.

Let's leave it at this: If you're writing non-fiction, tell the truth; if you can't or won't do that, then write fiction.

About Reading.

It's likely you have known how to read for a while now. It seems to be second nature after a while. You look at a set of letters on a page or a screen and your brain comprehends the meaning behind them. You piece the words and sentences and paragraphs together and make sense of them.

For the reading we will do in this program, we will ask you to do things a little differently. Instead of putting the words and sentences together to make sense of them, you'll be taking things apart. You'll be reading to determine what about the way the writer put the piece together works and what doesn't. Think of this as looking at writing as a writer. In the same way that a painter might look at a painting, studying the brush strokes and the shading and the colors, writers look at writing by studying the words and the sentences and the paragraphs.

As you take apart the paragraphs and sentences of a piece of writing, you aren't reading for enjoyment. Indeed, the question of whether or not you like something we read is almost irrelevant. Instead, you are reading to consider every seemingly innocent choice the writer made about words and phrases and sentences. This is close reading and most of us have to learn how to read this way.

Here are a few things to keep in your mind when you read:

- Read slowly and savor each word, phrase, and sentence. Wonder why the writer chose specific words and phrases. Pick apart sentences and consider what the word choices tell you about the narrator, the characters, the story itself.

- Wonder who is the narrator. Why is the narrator speaking to us and telling the story? What's in it for him or her?

- When a character does something in your story, whether it's a major act like joining the army during a time of war or some simple gesture like tossing a ball up and down in his hand, wonder what that tells you about that person. Ask why the writer would have the character do that.

- Where does the story take place? How does the writer describe it? What about the people and things and places in the story: What do they look like? Why do they look that way? What does it tell us?

- How do people speak and particularly how do they speak to each other? Does the dialogue seem realistic? What type of language do they use? Is it rough and tumble or sweet and sleek?

- Finally, what's the point of the story? What are we supposed to take away from our reading?

WRITING THE MILITARY EXPERIENCE

This is a book about writing the military experience. It is not about military writing. That is a whole different world. A U.S. Army pamphlet titled Effective Writing for Army Leaders said, *"the standard for Army writing is writing you can understand in a single rapid reading, and is generally free of errors in grammar, mechanics, and usage. Good Army writing is clear, concise, organized, and right to the point."* Orders and instructions need to be clear, concise, and complete. Writing about the military experience is different. As we said earlier, we write to create literature, to create an aesthetic experience for the reader. This is not easily done in the best of circumstances. But in writing the military experience, we face some additional obstacles.

War narratives have illuminated war's chaos, violence, and human suffering as well as its humor, irony, and the intense passions it can generate. In these works man's highest aspirations in the arts are inextricably fused with our deadliest creations. We set poetry, the *belles-lettres,* and creative non-fiction alongside chemical weapons, intercontinental missiles with thermonuclear warheads, and robotic drones. And in the process, we find a synthesis of imaginations used for vastly disparate ends.

Yet many writers feel that war is too difficult a subject to write about. How could one possibly address something on the scale of the Second World War—six years of war fought globally, over 60 million killed, the Holocaust—with mere words on the page? It's important to keep in mind that we are writing about the military experience, not specifically or exclusively about war. But nonetheless, war is part of the military experience, perhaps the seminal part.

As veterans or the family members of veterans we have a unique advantage over others in writing the military experience: our authority. We write from first-hand experience. As participants—combatant or family member irrespective—we create a literature *of war* rather than a literature *about war.*

Many believe that veterans have a responsibility to tell their stories and the larger story of wars to those who remained behind. This witnessing is a critical reason many veterans write: they feel they have a duty to do so; a duty either to their comrades who did not return or to the society that ordered them to go to war.

Some will argue that creating works of literature of or about war glorifies it and encourages the next generation to go to war rather than to do anything possible to stop it. Others have said that in the wake of so much killing in the 20th century, and in particular the Holocaust, that to create poetry or other works or art is barbaric.

These are powerful philosophical positions that we acknowledge, but neither challenge or support. We are here to write and to become better writers. As individuals, as writers, we face other tests. Some returning veterans find themselves unable to summon the words to describe what they have witnessed and participated in. Trauma alters the way the brain works, reducing the ability to express oneself verbally. So maybe writing is helpful in these cases.

But this also gets back to the idea that one cannot possibly describe a war to anyone who has not participated. Words are often not sufficient. But they are what we have. So we must make them work.

We must because we uniquely have the experience of the combatant in battle. It is to us to bear the report to those who come after, as Justice Holmes said. We must carry out with us the stories of the survivors, and of the dead. Ernest Hemingway's protagonist from *A Farewell to Arms*, Frederic Henry, says,

> *"I was always embarrassed by the words sacred, glorious, and sacrifice... I had seen nothing sacred, and the things that were glorious had no glory.... There were many words that you could not stand to hear and finally only the names of places had any dignity. Abstract words such as glory, honor, courage, or hallow were obscene beside the concrete names of villages."*

Again, words are not always sufficient, but they are all we have. We have to make them work. We have to try to give substance to abstractions like glory, honor, and valor, while we memorialize names like Belleau Wood, Normandy, Hue, and Fallujah.

In addition to these burdens, there are other challenges for those of us who write the military experience. As we discussed above, we are often writing about the most primal of emotions and urges. We might write about killing or fear, loneliness or hatred. There might be violence and brutality, or a grim determination in the face of unenviable odds. Sometimes there is shame. But there can also be moments of intense beauty and surprising gentleness.

This is not to say that writers working on non-military subject matter don't touch on these emotions and situations. But writing the military experience is different than writing about the struggle of a man against an animal, or an interpersonal conflict in a courtroom, or even a gang war in some post-apocalyptic urban landscape.

For one thing, we begin with a disadvantage other writers don't have: Many of our readers are poorly informed about the subject matter. In 2011, less than 1% of the American population served in the military. Of over 310 million Americans, only about 2.3 million were in uniform, including reservists. So over 99% of America is disengaged, divorced from the military and very likely ignorant of the traditions, language, humor, dangers, and sacrifices inherent in the service experience.

How do we bridge that divide? How do we show, tell, explain, document, honor, and expose the military experience? This is a big question that we will take apart and try to answer piece by piece. The technical question of how and when we should show or tell gets into aesthetic questions and technique. We will spend time on this question, but later.

We make an assumption here: that our writing will be read by others who do not know the military experience. So we can start with this question: How do we impart the sensation of something unique and specific? How much and what type of detail do we have to provide the reader about an event or situation or setting for an uninitiated audience to get it?

When we describe something from our military experience, it's smart and easy to fall back on language that is specific to the experience. This adds authority to our writing. But it is also very easy to slip into jargon, language that is peculiar to a profession or a trade. The language of today's profession of arms is ruled by jargon and acronyms. Some of this makes its way into the common vernacular—words like *humvee* and phrases like *good-to-go*, for example—but so much of what we say among ourselves is like a foreign language to outsiders.

It is occasionally purposefully so. We use euphemisms to obscure and to protect—*friendly fire, collateral damage*. But we can also very easily slip into the argot of the military briefing—

BMNT is at 0613; Class I, III, and V will be available in the LSA; ADA is OPCON, ROE weapons tight—or the patois of the specialist as a type of shorthand—*call the TOC and tell the S2 NCO there are three EPWs here; we had two other AOGs who were KIA.*

These all have significant meaning to someone initiated into the fraternity, but to the 99% of Americans who aren't in the club, this is gobbledygook. So it's important to limit the use of specialized language.

Consider the poem, *Trench Duty*, by Siegfried Sassoon:

> *Shaken from sleep, and numbed and scarce awake,*
> *Out in the trench with three hours' watch to take,*
> *I blunder through the splashing mirk; and then*
> *Hear the gruff muttering voices of the men*
> *Crouching in cabins candle-chinked with light.*
> *Hark! There's the big bombardment on our right*
> *Rumbling and bumping; and the dark's a glare*
> *Of flickering horror in the sectors where*
> *We raid the Boche; men waiting, stiff and chilled,*
> *Or crawling on their bellies through the wire.*
> *'What? Stretcher-bearers wanted? Some one killed?'*
> *Five minutes ago I heard a sniper fire:*
> *Why did he do it? ... Starlight overhead—*
> *Blank stars. I'm wide-awake; and some chap's dead.*

Sassoon uses simple words that everyone in that era would know. Today, we might not use *Boche* for German or the poetic *mirk* to describe a gloomy, dark place (mirk is an archaic usage that is today rendered as murky), but everything else is pretty clear. Our narrator is tired, it's the middle of the night; there is fighting, a bombardment off somewhere to our right; and then, suddenly, some chap is dead and there is a call for stretcher bearers; and there are questions.

Sassoon has used everyday words to express something quite specific: his experience of the death from a sniper's bullet of a soldier in a trench during the middle of clear night. Certainly a soldier of the era would be intimately familiar with this. But because he has chosen to use no military-specific language, the work can have meaning for a wider audience. It doesn't reduce the authenticity of the voice. I don't doubt that Sassoon actually did *blunder through the splashing mirk*.

And that word, blunder, is some choice. Why not stumble? It might more accurately describe what he's doing. Nonetheless, Sassoon chose blunder. Is he trying to make a wider statement? We'll come back to this poem later when we talk about narrative structure.

One final example on the point of how technical we need to get to describe the military experience. Richard McKenna, in his novel *The Sand Pebbles*, describes the protagonist's attempts at dismantling the ship's boiler. Holman is a U.S. Navy petty officer, Po-Han a Chinese coolie working for Holman in the boiler room of the USS San Pablo.

> *The engine fought back. The coupling nuts would not come loose. There were thirty of them, ten to a flange, each nut four inches across, and they were welded in their threads by the rust of fifty years. Po-han held the wrench steady and Holman swung the twenty-pound sledge until his wrists felt wooden and his fingers trembled and he could barely close his hands. In two hours, they got one nut off.*

> *"Po-han, we got to get smart about this,"* Holman said.

> *With ball peen hammers they beat the paint off all the nuts, hoping by the repeated small*

shocks to loosen the rust-bind in the threads. They dripped kerosene on the exposed bolt threads, hoping it would seep inside the nuts to loosen and lubricate. Then Holman sledged again.

There was an art to sledging. Amateurs used a full-arm swing and it was mostly noise and show. The best way was to move the sledge only about a foot, arms rigid and your right hand only a few inches from the hammer head, and swing your whole body from the ankles. You made your whole body into a battering ram with the sledge as the striking point, and you poured the fused momentum of bone, muscle and steel into what you hit. If what you hit did not yield, all the energy reflected back into you, and it jarred you to your heels.

McKenna knows what he's talking about here. He retired as a Chief Machinist Mate after serving in WWII and Korea. But even without knowing that, I trust what he has to say. When he tells me these four-inch wide nuts are welded into their threads by the rust of fifty years, I believe him. So when he starts to explain how Holman and Po-han go about trying to loosen the nuts before Holman goes back to sledging, I trust that they are doing the right thing. Then, he explains how one goes about sledging; there's an art to it, we learn. I will certainly approach the act of sledging differently from now on, knowing how amateurs do it—all noise and show. And there isn't a military specific bit of jargon anywhere.

Based on what we've seen thus far, it's safe to say that we don't need to explain how every nut and bolt of any operation worked for our readers to get it. It's important to use specific language, not jargon. There is a fine line between establishing your narrator as an expert and confusing your readers.

Now, about those readers—your audience. One of the early questions in this endeavor, right after *why do I want to write* and *what do I want to say*, should be *who am I writing this for.* Determining your audience is just as important as your subject matter. This will drive your structure and length certainly. But it will also drive things like word choice, the words you use and how you use them.

English has two main sources for words: German and Latin. They divide our language in half. Latinate words tend to describe the intellectual world; Germanic words, the physical. Latinate words tend to be longer, Germanic words shorter.

The words we choose and how we form them into clauses, phrases, and sentences determine our diction—either high or low. Generally, writers use high diction to give the impression of erudition (this is a very high diction, Latinate word) or a higher-class status. Low diction can impart a sense of groundedness, of directness, or of lower class status.

Here's an example of high diction:

> *When you came in the space was desultory, rectangular, warm after the drip of the winter night, and transfused with brown-orange dust that was light. It was shaped like the house a child draws. Three groups of brown limbs spotted with brass took dim high-lights from shafts that came from a bucket pierced with holes, filled with incandescent coke and covered in with a sheet of iron in the shape of a funnel. Two men, as if hierarchically smaller, crouched on the floor beside the brazier; four, two at each end of the hut drooped over the table in attitudes of extreme indifference. From the eaves above the parallelogram of black that*

was the doorway fell intermittent dripping of collected moisture, persistent, with glass-like intervals of musical sound. The two men squatting on their heels over the brazier —they had been miners—began to talk monotonously, without animation. It was as if one told the other long, long stories to which his companion manifested his comprehension or sympathy with animal grunts.

This is from Ford Madox Ford's war trilogy *Parade's End*. Ford opens the middle book, *No More Parades,* with this description filled with long, Latinate words like *desultory, transfused, incandescent, hierarchically, and monotonously*. It seems overly formal: *From the eaves above the parallelogram of black that was the doorway fell intermittent...* Now granted, this was written in 1926. But it is a good example of the use of high diction. It gives the reader a sense that the narrator or character is cultured, formally educated, maybe pretentious.

And here is low diction:

Snake had an antenna for trouble, and he suddenly realized that Austin was capable of producing it.

But Austin had already turned to Cannonball, who was standing knee-deep in the hole he had been digging, laughing at Phony's humor. "You! Black Marine. Where's your fields of fire?"

Cannonball started for a quick moment at what he believed to be a slur, then regained his amused grin, and glanced out across the rippling patty to his front. "Aw, everywhere, man."

Austin continued, bolstered by his first direct response. "What do you mean, 'everywhere'? Where's your PDF?"

Cannonball scratched his head, squinting. "Say wha-a-at?"

"Your PDF. Principal Direction of Fire. Don't you have a PDF?"

Cannonball waved a lithe arm at Austin, ignoring Snake's attempt to silence him. "Awww, ma-a-an. Don't give me none of that boot-camp shit. You ever been overrun? We don't shoot no 'principle direction' man, we shoot gooks."

Snake finally was able to position himself between Austin and the others. He smiled a conciliatory grin, "Hey listen, I don't know who you are but—"

"Who the hell are you?"

"I'm the squad leader here. Now-"

"Well, I'm Staff *Sergeant Austin, your new Platoon Sergeant, and* you *piss me off."*

This is from James Webb's novel *Fields of Fire* and, as you've seen, introduces Staff Sergeant Angus Austin, the new Platoon Sergeant. It's abrupt and direct. There are no big words, a few common grammatical errors, a bit of profanity. Webb uses this language to show us how combat Marine non-commissioned officers talk. It's salty and gruff. He throws in a bit of jargon—*PDF*—but lets the uninitiated reader off the hook but having his character explain it away in a very convincing fashion.

Somewhere in the space between these two worlds, lodged in the no-man's land that is neither high nor low, is middle diction. This is really just the way most people think and speak. It's not overly figurative or pedantic, nor is it slangy or jargony, or common and profanity-laced.

Consider this:

I sat up and looked around. The crowd had drawn back in a wide circle. They were staring at me. A woman yammered something I couldn't follow and pointed under the jeep. I bent down for a look. There, lying directly below my seat, was a hand grenade. The pin had been pulled. I straightened up and sat there for a while, barely breathing. Then I got out of the jeep and walked over to where everyone else was standing. We were still within the grenade's killing range, especially if it set off the gas tank, but I didn't think of that any more than the others had. I didn't have a thought in my head. We just stood there like a bunch of fools.

Sergeant Benet appeared at the edge of the crowd. "What's going on?" he said.

"There's a grenade under the jeep."

This is from Tobias Wolff's memoir, *In Pharaoh's Army*, and in it he gives us a big dose of neutral. There are no words here that wouldn't fit into a normal conversation. Well, assuming people talk every day about finding a hand grenade under their jeep. But you get the point.

So far we have looked at words, mostly. We've examined the question of just how much we should explain about the world for our readers to get it. We've looked just a bit into diction, high low and middle. We're ready to move onto more complex issues of how do we put our readers into a place that feels real? This is setting.

But before we move on, here's another note. At the end of each section from here on there will be some exercises to help you practice what we've learned. This is where you get to do some writing.

Exercises:

1. Specific language. Write a paragraph, no more than 150 words, explaining something you did most days in the military. Chose something specific like changing out a part, boresighting a tank main gun or filing a specific kind of report or action. Describe the work in as much detail as you think is necessary but stay away from jargon and other language that a non-military member would shake their head over. This doesn't need to be poetic. It just needs to be clear.

2. In about 200 words describe the space where the senior officers in your command worked. Use high diction.

3. Again, in about 200 words, describe someone you worked with. Use low diction.

SETTING

When and where your story takes place is as important a decision as any you will make as a writer. Some stories really have only one time and place they could plausibly occur—think about *Apollo 13* or *Bridge on the River Kwai*. But a psychological thriller can be just as thrilling in Antarctica or the Brazilian rain forest. A comedy of errors is probably just as funny set in New York during the blackout of 1977 as in Ephesus and Syracuse in the 15th century. Setting is all about time and place.

Setting can play a number of roles in your story. It can simply be the place where the real action happens between people. It can help you as the writer set mood. It can be an active player, shaping the action at times as much as any character in the story.

So how do we present setting? Sometimes, filmmakers use what are called establishing shots: You see a rat running along a wharf and pull back to see a clipper ship being loaded by men in breeches. Pull further back and you see the Tower of London. Okay, we know where we are and have a good idea of the world we're entering.

You could reverse the shot and show the earth view from outer space, close in to see the Eastern Seaboard of the United

States, then drill down to see New York City and finally a street scene in a dodgy neighborhood, some boys playing ball on hoops with no nets while some guy cruises slowly by in an Escalade, and there are no cops anywhere. Okay, again, we get it.

As writers we have the challenge of using words to create these images in our readers' minds. But we can use some of the same techniques filmmakers use. Hemingway, in his novel *A Farewell to Arms*, does a good job of drilling down to bring the readers into a place and time. His protagonist, Frederic Henry, is returning from the hospital after being wounded. He's been gone for a few weeks and is coming back to the village where he was staying when he was hit by mortar fragments.

> *When I came back to the front we still lived in that town. There were many more guns in the country around and the spring had come. The fields were green and there were small green shoots on the vines, the trees along the road had small leaves and a breeze came from the sea. I saw the town with the hill and the old castle above it in a cup in the hills with the mountains beyond, brown mountains with a little green on their slopes. In the town there were some new hospitals, you met British men and sometimes women, on the street, and a few more houses had been hit by shellfire. ...[I]found we still lived in the same house and that it all looked the same as when I left it. The door of the house was open, there was a soldier sitting on a bench outside in the sun, an ambulance was waiting by the side door and inside the door, as I went in, there was the smell of marble floors and hospital. It was all as I had left it except that now it was spring. ...*

> *The room I shared with the lieutenant Rinaldi looked out on the courtyard. The window was open, and my things hung on the*

*wall, the gas mask in an oblong tin can, the steel
helmet on the same peg. At the foot of the bed
was my flat trunk, and my winter boots, the
leather shiny with oil, were on the trunk. My
Austrian sniper's rifle with its blued octagon
barrel and the lovely dark walnut cheek fitted,
schutzen stock, hung over the two beds. ...*

So we start with a view of the surrounding countryside, then
the village, then the street and the house, finally the room where
he lived and his things. Hemingway tells us not only about the
village itself, but also gives us a sense of the feel of the town—he
says twice that things seem to be just as he left them, only now
it's spring and warmer. Not much happens here that advances
the story--this really is an establishing shot. Hemingway puts it
all up front and gets it out of the way, placing the reader and the
characters in time and setting so action can happen.

It's not always necessary to take up multiple paragraphs or
pages describing a place or a setting for a scene. James Michener
does a marvelous job of establishing setting in this clip from
Tales from the South Pacific:

*It was my first time down into the
compressed, clicking, bee-hive world of the
submariners. I never got used to the strange
noises. A head of steam pounding through the
pipes above my face would make me shudder
and gasp for air. Even Charlesworth had trouble
with his collar, which wasn't buttoned.*

Michener doesn't describe the submarine, but still gives us a
sense of it. He never uses the word claustrophobic, but he
creates the mood, he plants the idea with his words. He plays off
of the uniqueness of the setting for the narrator, on the noises
and the sense that things are right in your face. He chooses
words like *compressed, clicking, and bee-hive* to put us into a
place where we are certain to feel claustrophobic—choosing to
use words that start with the same sounds like compressed and

clicking might even put the word claustrophobic into our heads. Notice how those pipes are right above your face, so your sense of personal space is disrupted while you're gasping for air. Finally, he seals the deal with the image of someone feeling like he's choking on his collar, which isn't even buttoned.

Similarly, Philip Caputo deftly chooses his words and images to set us into a frame of mind and to make us feel the discomfort, the pain of humping on a combat patrol in his novel, *A Rumor of War*.

> *The company is tramping down a dirt road past a Catholic church built long ago by French missionaries. Its Gothic style looks out of place in this Asian landscape. Its walls are made of a dark, volcanic-looking rock. The courtyard is enclosed by a stone fence which bougainvillea covers like bunting and there is a crucifix atop the arched gate. We are marching in a double file through a pall of dust raised by our boots. The dust drifts slowly away from the road and sifts down on the courtyard, dulling the brilliance of the bougainvillea. It is an extremely hot day, hotter than any we have yet experienced. We have been told that the temperature is over one hundred and ten degrees, but the figure is meaningless. The cruelty of this sun cannot be measured by an instrument. Head bowed, a machine gunner in front of me is walking with his weapon braced across the back of his shoulders, one hand hanging over the muzzle and the other over the butt, so that his shadow resembles the Christ figure atop the gate of the church. Farther on, the road runs past a stretch of low, grassy hills and flooded rice patties. A deserted village lies ahead, a little more than halfway to our objective, the tea plantation.*

So Caputo has us tramping, marching in the dust on a day so hot that instruments of measurement are meaningless. The church is made of *volcanic-looking rock*, in case the idea of the hot sun wasn't bad enough, now we're thinking about volcanoes. The guy just in front of us, the machine gunner, mirrors Christ on the cross with all of the agony and suffering associated with that image. The only thing that could possibly bring beauty to this scene, the bougainvillea, is being covered in the dust our marching is kicking up. The same dust we're choking on. Oh, and there are hills to climb ahead. They're surrounding the rice patties we're going to have to slog through. It's going to be a long day and no one has even shot at us yet.

Sometimes the setting can actually take on more prominence and become an actor, influencing the action, driving the storyline, advancing the plot. In his epic memoir, *The Seven Pillars of Wisdom*, T.E. Lawrence takes us into the Arabian desert on an extended campaign to disrupt Turkish supply lines along the Medina Railroad:

> There had been long rolls of thunder all morning in the hills, and the two peaks, Serd and Jasim, were wrapped in folds of dark blue and yellow vapour, which looked motionless and substantial. At last I saw that part of the yellow cloud off Serd was coming slowly against the wind in our direction, raising scores of dust devils before its feet.
>
> The cloud was nearly as high as the hill. While it approached, two dust-spouts, tight and symmetrical chimneys, advanced, one on the right and one on the left of its front. Dakhil-Allah responsibly looked ahead and to each side for shelter, but saw none. He warned me that the storm would be heavy.
>
> When it got near, the wind, which had been scorching our faces with its hot breathlessness,

changed suddenly; and, after waiting a moment, blew bitter cold and damp upon our backs. It also increased greatly in violence, and at the same time the sun disappeared, blotted out by thick rags of yellow air over our heads. We stood in a horrible light, ochreous and fitful. The brown wall of cloud from the hills was now very near, rushing changelessly upon us with a loud grinding sound. Three minutes later it struck, wrapping about us a blanket of dust and stinging grains of sand, twisting and turning in violent eddies, and yet advancing eastward at the speed of a strong gale.

We had put our camels' backs to the storm, to march before it: but these internal whirling winds tore our tightly-held cloaks from our hands, filled our eyes, and robbed us of all sense of direction by turning our camels right or left from their course. Sometimes they were blown completely round: once we clashed helplessly together in a vortex, while large bushes, tufts of grass, and even a small tree were torn up by the roots in dense waves of the soil about them, and driven against us, or blown over our heads with dangerous force. We were never blinded—it was always possible to see for seven or eight feet to each side—but it was risky to look out, as, in addition to the certain sand-blast, we never knew if we should not meet a flying tree, a rush of pebbles, or a spout of grass-laden dust.

This storm lasted for eighteen minutes, and then leaped forward from us as suddenly as it had come. Our party was scattered over a square mile or more, and before we could rally, while we, our clothes and our camels were yet smothered in dust, yellow and heavy with it from head to foot, down burst torrents of thick rain and muddied us to the skin. The valley began to run in plashes of water, and Dakhil-Allah urged us across it quickly. The wind chopped once more, this time to the north, and the rain came driving before it in harsh sheets of spray. It beat through our woolen cloaks in a moment, and moulded them and our shirts to our bodies, and chilled us to the bone.

Lawrence's campaign is halted by the storm. In this case, the setting, the physical environment in which the story takes place, becomes an actor. It plays a role in the storyline. Lawrence's description is both beautiful and terrifying. Small trees are torn up by the roots and fly through the air; the raiding party is scattered over a square mile or more; amid sudden torrents of rain comes the threat of a flash flood; the men are so covered in dirt and dust that when the rain comes they are muddied to the skin.

*

This is a good place to begin looking at description. There's all this stuff in your stories: stuff your characters do, the stuff they wear and drive and fly and throw and catch and sleep under and through, the stuff sitting around on tables and the tables the stuff is sitting on. Lots of stuff. Your job as a writer is to describe that stuff.

There are any number of ways to describe something. The simplest is to just describe it directly: *a gray metal folding chair*. This gives us a pretty clear idea of what it is: a chair that folds, that is made of metal, and that is painted gray.

But we don't get much of an idea about what the chair is doing in the setting. We probably wouldn't bother to describe the chair if it didn't have a purpose in the story. That might only be to decorate a space, to show the readers what's in the room as a way of demonstrating some facet of our character's life or to demonstrate some plot point. But it has a purpose.

In the piece out of *A Rumor of War* we looked at earlier, Caputo takes the time to describe the church for a few reasons: He needs to use the Christ-on-the-Cross metaphor; he gives us the volcano reference by describing the stones from which the church is made, it serves to remind us that others have been here before us.

When Caputo chooses to say that the machine gunner *resembles* Christ on the cross, he is helping us to understand one thing, the image of the machine gunner, by giving us something else we can compare it to, the image of Christ on the Cross. This is a metaphor.

Metaphors compare two things side by side so that we will better understand one of the items. Of course, because there are two objects or actions under consideration in a metaphor, there have to be two parts to it: They are the tenor and the vehicle. The tenor is the item being described or compared. The vehicle is what the writer uses to define or describe the tenor.

For example:

> *The horse that Big Ace was riding was nice
> and plump like a merchant's daughter.*

This is from Isaac Babel's Red Cavalry story, *Konkin*. In it, Babel tells how he captured a general officer. The "Big Ace" is the general, but specifically Babel is describing the general's horse in terms his readers would certainly understand: plump like a merchant's daughter. The horse in this case is the tenor of the metaphor and the merchant's daughter is the vehicle.

In one of Babel's other Red Cavalry stories, *My First Goose*, he describes Savitsky, the commander of the Sixth Division, like this:

> *He rose—his breeches purple, his crimson cap cocked to the side, his medal pinned to his chest—splitting the hut in two like a banner splitting the sky. He smelled of perfume and the nauseating coolness of soap. His long legs looked like two girls wedged to their shoulders into riding boots.*

There is a lot happening here. First, Savitsky is obviously a big man. When he stands up, it's as if someone has raised a banner or a flag. I once heard someone described as being so big he blocked out the sun; this seems a similar metaphor. But Babel doesn't stop there. He says the man's legs look like two girls who have been stuffed into riding boots. This is quite an image.

One technical note, these are actually similes because they make the comparison of the two by using the words *like* or *as* (you could argue that Caputo's use of *resembles* in his metaphor makes it a simile, I suppose). All similes are metaphors, they compare two items, but not all metaphors are similes because they don't all use *like* or *as*.

Metaphors don't necessarily have to be limited to one or two lines. A writer can stretch the metaphor out through a paragraph or even a story. Continuing a metaphor through a few lines is an extended metaphor.

Consider this Wilfred Owen poem from 1917:

> *Anthem for Doomed Youth*
>
> *What passing-bells for these who die as cattle?*
> *Only the monstrous anger of the guns.*
> *Only the stuttering rifles' rapid rattle*
> *Can patter out their hasty orisons.*
> *No mockeries for them; no prayers nor bells,*
> *Nor any voice of mourning save the choirs, —*
> *The shrill, demented choirs of wailing shells;*
> *And bugles calling for them from sad shires.*
> *What candles may be held to speed them all?*

Not in the hands of boys, but in their eyes
Shall shine the holy glimmers of goodbyes.
The pallor of girls' brows shall be their pall;
Their flowers the tenderness of patient minds,
And each slow dusk a drawing-down of blinds.

Once you know that passing bells are the church bells rung for a funeral and orisons are prayers, this is more accessible. Owen's opening metaphor here is to compare the sounds of artillery and rifles to church bells and prayers. He extends the metaphor by comparing the shriek of shells passing overhead and buglers' calls (perhaps playing The Last Post or, in the United States, Taps) to the voices of a choir.

It's also possible to create an entire story where things represent other things. This is called allegory. William Golding's *Lord of the Flies,* for example, is deeply allegorical. Ralph and Piggy, Jack and Simon, even the conch, are symbolic, representing ideas, principles, tenets, beliefs, and so on.

*

Now back to setting for one last point. Before we move on, it's worth noting that setting is important in both fiction and non-fiction. Setting is one of the ways that you as a writer can set the mood of a piece. Mood is the atmosphere of the story. The classic opening line cliché, "It was a dark and stormy night" comes to mind. But we'll try to avoid clichés. Think of the short paragraph from Michener above. Michener sets a mood of claustrophobia through his descriptions of the space and its effect on people.

In his short story "Ball of Fat," Guy de Maupassant tells us how things feel in the French town of Rouen just before and after the town changes hands, when the Germans take over, during the Franco-Prussian war.

A profound calm, a frightful, silent
expectancy had spread over the city. Many of the
heavy citizens, emasculated by commerce,

anxiously awaited the conquerors, trembling lest their roasting spits or kitchen knives be considered arms. All life seemed stopped; shops were closed, the streets dumb. Sometimes an inhabitant, intimidated by this silence, moved rapidly along next to the walls. The agony of waiting made them wish the enemy would come.

In the afternoon of the day which followed the departure of the French troops, some Uhlans, coming from one knows not where, crossed the town with celerity. Then, a little later, a black mass descended the side of St. Catharine, while two other invading bands appeared by the way of Darnetal and Boisguillaume. ...

Some orders of the commander, in a foreign, guttural voice, reached the houses which seemed dead and deserted, while behind closed shutters, eyes were watching these victorious men, masters of the city, of fortunes, of lives, through the "rights of war." The inhabitants, shut up in their rooms, were visited with the kind of excitement that a cataclysm, or some fatal upheaval of the earth, brings to us, against which all force is useless. For the same sensation is produced each time that the established order of things is overturned, when security no longer exists, and all that protect the laws of man and of nature find themselves at the mercy of unreasoning, ferocious brutality.

The trembling of the earth crushing the houses and burying an entire people; a river overflowing its banks and carrying in its course the drowned peasants, carcasses of beeves, and girders snatched from roofs, or a glorious army massacring those trying to defend themselves, leading others prisoners, pillaging in the name of the sword and thanking God to the sound of the cannon, all are alike frightful scourges which disconnect all belief in eternal justice, all the confidence that we have in the protection of Heaven and the reason of man. ...

After some time, as soon as the first terror disappears, a new calm is established. ...

The town even took on, little by little, its ordinary aspect. The French scarcely went out, but the Prussian soldiers grumbled in the streets. ...

There was nevertheless, something in the air, something subtle and unknown, a strange, intolerable atmosphere like a penetrating odor, the odor of invasion. It filled the dwellings and the public places, changed the taste of the food, gave the impression of being on a journey, far away, among barbarous and dangerous tribes.

That sort of sums it up nicely, doesn't it—*something in the air?* De Maupassant gives us the evolution of the feeling in the town and tells us why, *"for the same sensation is produced each time that the established order of things is overturned."* But he shows as well as he tells: *Shops were closed, the streets dumb.* Even though all of this occurs in the first couple pages of the story, it's not just an establishing shot. The setting here has a role to play. It establishes us, the readers and the characters, into a place and time. In this place, the setting—inside the city waiting for the victorious Prussians to enter—causes the characters to act and react in a certain way, to flee. But it also gives us a palpable sensation of fear, anxiety, of dread. The town, the setting, has become a character in the story. Du Maupassant deftly takes us inside the town's head and sets the mood of the story.

Finally, setting should influence your characters. The place and time—think of the environment and even the cultural mores of the time—really must have some influence on your characters. In A.E.W. Mason's classic novel *The Four Feathers*, the protagonist is a young army officer who resigns his commission and is thought to be a coward. The cultural mores of the time create conditions where four contemporaries each send the protagonist, Harry Feversham, a white feather signaling their affirmation of his cowardice. If this story had been written in 2002 rather than 1902, four feathers might mean little to Harry. But in that setting, in Victorian England, his honor is everything. Setting—time and place—has influenced him.

At one point late in the story, Mason has Feversham allow himself to be captured by the Sudanese so that he might help a former comrade escape from a notoriously brutal prison, the House of Stone. The setting inside the prison is a brutal, filthy world unto itself. The test for Feversham and his English colleague is to survive in a world utterly unlike their own and maintain their mores as much as their lives. The setting, in this case, challenges the characters but does not prevail—unlikely in an English novel of the day of course.

But now, some exercises.

1. Choose a setting. It can be anywhere, anytime of your choosing. Catalog its details. The geography (even indoors), what is the physical layout of the place? The time both in terms of period and day,is it the 14th century or the 21st century? Is it morning? If so, what do the sun, the sky, and all the objects in the scene look like? Keep this up with people and weather. Describe color, shape, temperature, sensation, mood.

2. Now, write a scene of great grief in that setting. Pay attention to how the details of setting help you animate the actions of the characters. How does the external world influence the internal world of your characters?

3. Now write another short scene, in the same location, only make this one where a character feels longing maybe even lust. Again, how can you make the external world influence your characters' internal life?

CHARACTER

The people in your story really are the most important part. It's possible to write a story about a mountain or a chair or the wind, but it probably isn't going to be very interesting until you show your reader all the obstacles the team of mountain climbers struggle to overcome to get to the base-camp and the inter-personal struggles among the group to determine who actually gets to summit the mountain first, or that the chair was the one on which General Grant sat in his muddy boots to accept General Lee's surrender, or how the wind rattling the windows in the old house late at night reminds the woman of the time in the old country when vampires actually did exist. It is people that make a good story. Those people are your characters. Your job as a writer is to create characters and put them into situations where they can interact.

Let me make a point here: This creating characters business may seem to only apply to fiction writers, but that's not true. Non-fiction writers don't have to create characters, but they have to understand the roles people play in their stories. Non-fiction writers have to populate their stories with characters—who happen to be real—and to fit those characters into certain roles. So, non-fiction writers, stick around.

Let's start with a basic inventory of the characters you might need. The protagonist is the lead character, the one the reader should think the most about. But is one character enough? Well, it's not impossible, but it's awfully hard to write an interesting story in which there is only one character. The tale of Robinson Crusoe is pretty interesting: Crusoe is marooned on an island, he rescues Friday from cannibal slavers and the two go on to share adventures on the island for 28 years. The tale that inspired DeFoe to write Crusoe, that of Scottish Sailor Alexander Selkirk, isn't as much fun: Selkirk is marooned on an island alone for four years. The more interesting story is one in which people interact. So you might want another character: the antagonist, the character in opposition to or threatening the protagonist.

Sometimes, this is all you need, two characters. Playwrights call two-character plays two-handers and they are typically sparse and potent with taut dialogue. The difficulties in this type of work are manifest: Your two characters are the only ones you can give life to and they must animate the entire story. The world you create and their interaction is what must sustain the entire work. It's a lot of pressure on two characters and on you as the writer. So you might want to create other characters.

There are, of course, multiple character types. They can be as simple as good guys and bad guys, but there are also role players, characters who serve a purpose in the plot and, once they have served that purpose, can be done away with. There are archetypes: hero, the mother or father figure, the underdog. There are also stereotypes and clichés: the ignorant hick southern cop, the cynical wisecracking guy from Brooklyn, the fallen woman with the heart of gold.

Vladimir Propp, a Russian/Soviet structuralist, analyzed Russian folk tales and determined there were seven basic character types that appeared with regularity. Now, obviously not all of us intend to write Russian folk tales, in fact I assume very few of us do, but the models are worth looking at.

—Propp's protagonist is usually a hero. These are not always one in the same character. A hero is an archetypal character. In fairy tales, the hero is usually the guy who slays the dragon and gets the princess. But the archetype demands the person face some grave danger for other than personal gain. There should be courage, self-sacrifice, and some moral challenge involved. In wartime, and in war stories, the idea is the same, that's why the phrase "above and beyond the call of duty" is in the citation for every Medal of Honor award. The recipient does something above and beyond what is expected and becomes a hero.

—The antagonist to Propp is the villain, another archetype. This is the main foil to the protagonist/hero. He or she is the person who presents the biggest obstacle to the protagonist reaching his objectives or goals.

—The dispatcher or tasker. Propp found that there was usually a character in the story who sends the hero on the quest. This might be a person who simply notifies the hero of a need or of a problem (let's say it's a dragon) or the person who actually instructs the hero to go and slay the dragon.

—A helper. Everyone needs a little help now and then and Propp provides it for us, and for the hero, in the form of the helper. (This would be Friday in *Robinson Crusoe*, above.)

—The prize or the princess. In fairy tales or folk tales, the hero is often on the quest to gain access to something or someone. It's very often the princess but it might be something like the Holy Grail.

—The father/owner of the prize. This might be the Duke or the King whose daughter is missing or endangered, or it might be the owner of the prize if the prize is an object that must be returned.

—The donor. Often the hero and his helper need some magical amulet or a piece of knowledge in order to carry out the task. This comes from the donor.

—The false hero. Sometimes, there is a fraudulent hero in the story who takes credit for the hero's work or somehow otherwise is in position to steal the prize.

These are archetypes and maybe it's hard to place them in context outside of the folk tale. So let's try to place them into another setting. What might be the furthest story line imaginable from a Russian folk tale: a Bond movie. Obviously the hero is Bond, James Bond. M is the dispatcher; he (now she) dispatches bond to destroy the villain. Bond stops by to visit Q, the donor, who gives 007 lots of amulets in the form of gadgets and toys. The Bond girls might look like the prize, but the prize is actually saving the world, so in many cases the Bond girl is an antagonist, standing between Bond and the prize, or the helper, getting Bond to the finish line.

OK, let's leave the analogy and talk about how characters are developed and presented in a story. Take a minute and think about some of your friends and family. You know some of these people really, really well. You know what they like and don't like, whether or not they are likely to be reliable in a sticky situation, their bad habits. They are, in your mind, complete people.

There are other people you know but not as well. Maybe you know a little bit about their background--They might be from Montana, or is it North Dakota? You might know something about their habits, but not too much.

This is how characters in your story exist as well. Some of them you will spend an enormous amount of time with and others you'll only need to wander into a scene for a moment, perhaps to deliver a line or a pizza. The characters you know well and you spend lots and lots of time with are fully formed. They have lives, filled with needs and flaws and embarrassing habits. They are complex and will surprise the reader; they may even surprise you the author. They are multidimensional and, thus, round.

The less interesting characters are flat. These are simple creatures. They don't really need to have lives or flaws or embarrassing habits. Maybe they serve a minor purpose, a cab driver who gives your protagonist a bit of advice and then drives away. Or maybe they simply take up space in a scene, a crying baby and flustered mother sitting next to you at the bus stop. Maybe they don't need to be filled out because you just need a stereotypical southern policeman to put your protagonist into a bad situation. These characters are one dimensional, thus flat.

Going back to our Bond analogy, the villain is almost always flat. You recognize him the moment you see him. He doesn't surprise you, except maybe by doing that stupid thing of allowing Bond to repeatedly escape rather than simply killing 007 off when he can. The dispatcher M and donor Q are flat characters, too. But the Bond girls, while instantly recognizable, are often round characters. One of them is likely to surprise you by changing sides. They have complexities.

That Bond girl who changes sides is a dynamic character; she undergoes change in the course of the story. One of the defining aspects of a novel is character development—the evolution of character over the course of the book. Usually it is the protagonist who undergoes the change, and the story is about how he or she is changed and by what. Static characters in a story do not change or evolve.

We should think for a minute or two about how to create characters. If you're writing non-fiction this isn't a problem. In non-fiction, your characters are real people doing real things. You simply have to find a way to explain them to our readers. But a fiction writer begins with *tabula rasa*—a blank slate—and builds from there.

There are lots of ways to develop a character. Some writers simply look within themselves to create a similar character or find elements of a character. This autobiographical method has great benefit in that you might be the person in the world you know best. You the writer understand, or should understand, anyway, what makes you the person tick, what drives your decisions, what your needs and desires are.

From there, you the writer simply have to put some aspect of you the person into a functional character in the story. This doesn't necessarily imply that a writer uses him or herself as the complete model for a character, although that has been done, even in fiction. Instead, an author selects traits or habits, sensations or desires, as models for a fictional character.

Some writers use a biographical method of developing characters. They look around themselves and choose characters from among the people they observe. The best technique for doing this is to create characters by fusing elements of character—style, manner, speech, gait, shape, and so on—from numerous people into one character. This fusion helps to create more interesting characters because most people lack the full array of qualities you the writer are looking for in a character.

There are some other tested methods of developing characters.

—Look to the classics. Plumb the depths of classical literature for models. Study how Achilles and Agamemnon act, build a character around Clytemnestra or Penelope, pinch a few traits from Lear or Prince Hal. All of us learn from other writers, so we're not talking about plagiarism so long as you don't directly copy a character from one author's work into yours.

—The seven deadly sins. Since the beginning of time, writers have used archetypal models for characters that are built around single attributes. In medieval times, playwrights created theatrical interludes we now refer to as morality plays. These are broadly allegorical works where a protagonist represents man or mankind and other characters are personifications of vices and virtues, or of moral ideals.

It is difficult to make fully developed characters out of single virtues or vices, though. Take the 1960s TV show *Gilligan's Island,* for example. Think of each of the characters as representing one or more of the seven deadly sins. Lust: Ginger Grant; Gluttony: the Skipper; Greed: Thurston Howell III; Sloth: Mrs. Howell; Envy: Maryann; Anger: also the Skipper; Pride: the Professor. That leaves us with Gilligan, who might be a bumbling Everyman or maybe the Devil.

—Whole cloth. Perhaps the best way to develop characters is to simply make them up out of whole cloth, which means to create them from nothing. You should have an idea around which you are building your story. As you're thinking through the outline of the plot, you'll necessarily have to think through the characters you need to make the plot work.

But archetypal characters work well in certain kind of stories operating within certain rules sets, but not everyone's experience (in non-fiction) or everyone's story (fiction) will conform to their rigidity. Stories that operate in an environment of stress, confusion, and danger seem to live and operate outside of the restrictive bounds of archetype. These stories get to the core of what character, a human being, really is.

These stories and these characters demand another way to approach character development. In this territory you need to define character more precisely than archetypes allow. You might use two keywords to help you in this: agenda and psychology. What is it that your character really wants or needs in this story (agenda); what are the elements of your character's personality, background and psyche that help and hinder the quest.

*

This is a good point to shift a bit and talk about *showing* versus *telling*. We identified this as a question in the second chapter when we pondered how much detail we need to provide for a reader to understand the military experience. You provide that detail by either demonstrating it in action or simply describing it— showing or telling.

In every writing course ever taught, in innumerable discussions among writers, this has been a subject of contention. It is a matter of technique, of aesthetics, of authorial choice. Do you as an author show your character doing something as a way of illustrating some character trait or do you simply tell your reader the character did this or is like that?

Well, it depends. As broad outline, you could think about it like this: If you're writing about your protagonist and the trait you want to expose is one that is critical to the plot, show it. If it's a minor, flat character who isn't going to be around for long, you can probably tell it.

An important corollary to this decision is this: If you make your character do something, it should be for a purpose. You make your character take action because it advances your story and it demonstrates some piece of your character's personality that you want exposed.

Once again, we've gone a while without an example, so let's jump into *Catch-22*. The protagonist, Captain John Yossarian, is a bombardier in a B-25. Yossarian's position in the aircraft is in a plexiglass nose cone, cantilevered out in front, even further out than the pilot, separated from the rest of the crew, and any escape hatch, by a tight crawlway.

> *The crawlway was a narrow, square, cold tunnel hollowed out beneath the flight controls, and a large man like Yossarian could squeeze through only with difficulty. ...*

> *The crawlway was Yossarian's lifeline to outside from a plane about to fall, but Yossarian swore at it with seething antagonism, reviled it as an obstacle put there by providence as part of the plot that would destroy him. ...*

So this is a bit of a set-up. Heller is describing the space; it is exactly what Heller's narrator has described it as: an obstacle to Yossarian's wants and needs—his individual survival. But he's setting us up for something, right? Then we get this:

> *...the only thing that kept him from abandoning his post under fire and scurrying back through the crawlway like a yellow-bellied rat was his unwillingness to entrust the evasive action out of the target area to anybody else. There was nobody else in the world that he would honor with so great a responsibility. There was nobody he knew who was so big a coward. Yossarian was the best in the squadron at evasive action, but he had no idea why."*

Heller tells us how Yossarian feels about himself here. He considers himself the biggest coward he knows. But he stays in position to conduct the mission of evasive action—guiding the pilot out of the area while under fire—because he trusts no one else with the responsibility, that of keeping the crew (and primarily Yossarian) alive. So we've been set up: Heller has given us the space, the character's needs and desires, and an obstacle or two. Now he can put things in motion. He can put together a scene in which we get to see Yossarian in action. This scene takes pace about 100 pages later in the novel, during a bombing run to Bologna.

> *Heavy flak was everywhere! He had been lulled, lured and trapped and there was nothing he could do but sit there like an idiot and watch the ugly black puffs smashing up to kill him. ...*

> *He could hear the hollow* boom-boom-boom-boom *of the flak pounding all around him in overlapping measures of four, the sharp, piercing* crack! *of a shell exploding suddenly very close by. His head was busting with a thousand dissonant impulses as he prayed for the bombs to drop. He wanted to sob. The engines droned on monotonously like a fat, lazy fly. At last the indices on the bombsight crossed,*

tripping away the 500-pounders one after the other. The plane lurched upward buoyantly with the lightened load. Yossarian bent away from the bombsight crookedly to watch the indicator on his left. When the pointer touched zero, he closed the bomb bay doors and, over the intercom, at the top of his voice shrieked, "Turn right hard!"

Heller has given us a setting, action, and some hints at Yossarian's state of mind: He prays, he wants to sob, he shrieks at the top of his voice. This is a very telling moment. Yossarian is acutely aware that in the war there are many people who want to do him harm, most immediately those responsible for "the ugly black puffs smashing up to kill him. " But he does his job, guiding the aircraft over the target and does his best to put the bombs on target. Once the bombs are away, though, he goes all out to make sure his aircraft survives to deliver him back to base. Because of his determination to survive, he has become the squadron's expert at avoiding death, instructing McWatt precisely how to corkscrew the aircraft through the sky to avoid the flak.

Still, Heller's narrator tells us that Yossarian has no idea why he is the best. Does he lack self-awareness? He realizes, or at least believes, he is the biggest coward he knows. The narrator may simply be pointing out an inconsistency in Yossarian. But it seems that Heller is also showing us an inconsistency in our expectations. Yossarian tells us he's a coward, but yet he goes up in the bomber every time he is told to and does his job. He does it well. We expect a coward to behave differently.

Heller has shown us Yossarian's motivation: to survive. And he has laid a series of obstacles in his way: flak, the crawlway, often Aarfy who comes into Yossarian's space blocking the crawlway. Heller chooses to tell us about things that create problems for Yossarian. He describes the crawlway and tells us how Yossarian feels about it, and thus why it is important. He chooses to show us Yossarian in action in order to let us observe and judge for ourselves what kind of person Yossarian really is. This might be the best model for when to show and when to tell: Show the profound and tell the mundane.

Beyond the technical point of show versus tell, Heller is providing us with information about Yossarian's motivation. Whenever we put a character into action, we have an opportunity to demonstrate somehow what motivates our character.

For Yossarian, the primary motivation is relatively simple: to survive. But for other characters in other stories, it's not always quite so clear. Most people are motivated by a variety of issues, some of which might carry the weight of life and death while many won't.

Kelly Kennedy's book, *They Fought for Each Other,* detailed the battles, external and internal, fought by an army infantry company in Iraq. Kennedy, who served as a soldier in the Gulf War and Somalia, understood that it wasn't the quest for glory that pushed PFC Ross McGinnis to jump on a grenade inside a humvee but rather his love for the other soldiers in the vehicle that day. When, after a few weeks of intense fighting, a platoon refused to go out on patrol, it wasn't cowardice that drove them but rather the knowledge that even as a unit the soldiers were unlikely to successfully steward their emotions, they feared they would lash out at the local civilian population and commit atrocities. Decisions like these are driven by an extremely complex set of motivations, a strong brew of anger, fear, integrity, hatred, bitterness and love. These are the emotions and choices that you have to understand and then make real and relevant to your readers.

The questions remain: How do you as a writer develop a sense of how your character would react in a certain situation and how do you convey that to the reader in a way that the reader completely believes that your character would act or react as you have described?

First of all, you the writer have to fully understand the character. Some writers actually catalogue the character's personality and history, creating a list of traits, habits, and tics that define the character. You might start a list like this for each of your major characters. (I'll give you a starting place at the end of this chapter.) I know a successful writer (eight books both non-fiction and fiction, plus twenty or so years as a journalist) who tells me he actually carries on conversations with his main characters in an attempt to get to know them. You'll have to find the techniques that work for you.

You will have to show the person exhibiting a range of emotions and actions so that when the climax arrives, what your character does may be a surprise but not wholly out of character or nonsensical.

One helpful way of getting to know your characters—and of introducing them to your readers—is to remember how we view real people. We watch what a person does; actions define. We listen to what the person says; words have meaning. We pay particular attention to the difference between words and deeds; this is the level of irony. We pay attention to how a person looks, how they present to the world in terms of clothes, personal style, and so on. We also consider the things and people a person surrounds himself with—these are choices. Finally, we like to know what a person thinks. Remember that thinking is an action. It is, in your story, an on-the-page process of how your character figures things out and views the world.

Exercises:

1. Make a catalog list of traits, habits, tics, and the like of someone you know well or of a (round) character in a piece of fiction you know well. Catalog the person's height, weight, eye color. Describe his or her hair; Is it long or short curly or straight, bobbed or pony-tailed? What kind of clothes is she wearing? What's in his pockets? What would that person say her favorite movie or flavor of ice cream was? Does she have a birthmark? Scars? Where and how did they get there? What

really makes this person happy or sad? What's their greatest fear? Does this person hoard a secret? What is it? What would make her laugh out loud or him cry in public? Who broke his heart in high school? What does her voice sound like?

2. Put that person into a situation where she or he is under stress. If this is fiction, make them sit in the car while a cop walks slowly up to the car window after pulling him or her over on a dark road at night. If it is a person you know, put them into a situation that is realistic for them. How does the person react? What's going on in his head? Take about 500 to 750 words.

3. Describe how the person you've written about in number 2 might act in the moments before she or he has the chance to realize their greatest dream or biggest fear. Again, what anxieties fill their head?

4. Think about two opposing traits a character might exhibit. Consider a complex character who might exhibit relatively equal amounts of both. Make a list of strengths and weaknesses that might follow from these character traits and then write a scene in which your character has to contend with his or her weaknesses and rely on strengths to make good on the agenda.

POINT OF VIEW

The people in a story, the characters, need a voice and you the author give this to them. You decide how your narrator will tell the story. This decision sets the Point of View, the position from which your story is told. We discussed folktales and fairy tales in the last chapters with the discussion of archetypal characters. In those forms, authors used characters as generic stand-ins for universal characteristics of human behavior. But few of us are writing folk tales. We need more.

At the turn of the 20th century, philosophers and psychologists—led by William James and Sigmund Freud—began describing the emotional processes and psychological development of individuals and how childhood influences shaped adult behavior. Freud's specific influence may have been greater on literary criticism and analysis than on authors, but for our purpose, post-Freud, there grew in literature a greater imperative on individual experience and distinct points of view.

Your role as an author is to decide the point of view. Is the story told by an omniscient, God-like being with the ability to know all, see all and tell all? Or is the story told by a single person with the myopia of being in the middle of the action and without the ability to pull back and get a larger picture? Point of view isn't simply the voice the narrator or the characters use, it is the psychological structure, the perspective that allows the reader to view them as human.

Lots of stories are told in the first person. The narrator says "I did this and they did that to me." Take a look at this paragraph from Isaac Babel's Red Cavalry story, "*Konkin*":

> *So there we were making mincemeat of the Poles at Belaya Tserkov. So much so that the trees were rattling. I'd been hit in the morning, but managed to keep on buzzing, more or less. The day, from what I remember, was toppling toward evening. I got cut off from the brigade commander, and was left with only a bunch of five proletarian Cossacks tagging along after me. All around me everyone's hugging each other with hatchets, like priests from two villages, the sap's slowly trickling out of me, my horse has pissed all over itself. Need I say more?*

Because Babel chose the first person point of view, he can tell the story from the standpoint of a single person speaking directly to the reader. This gives a sense of immediacy. It makes the story seem personal and allows the reader to enter the world of the narrator. "*So there we were,*" he says, "*making mincemeat of the Poles.*" But were they really making mincemeat of the Poles? That's the narrator's opinion. It may or may not be accurate.

The first person POV may give the reader reason to doubt the narrator's objectivity and reliability. What you're reading is the narrator's point of view, the narrator's opinion—which may or may not be accurate. As a reader, you can analyze (psychology, here again) why the narrator is telling you this. Are his or her reasons noble or shameful?

As a writer, there are some advantages and disadvantages to using first person. On the plus side, you just tell the story as you imagine your narrator would—in a single voice. On the down side, it forces you to present actions from only one angle—you're restricted to a single point of entry into any scene. Babel asks, *"Need I say more?"* Well, maybe.

Sometimes you will need to say more. Sometimes you might want to give the reader some distance from the character, or you might need to allow the character some privacy, or provide just a bit of distance between the narrator and the character. Frederic Manning, in his Roman-a-Clef, *Her Privates We,* uses the third person point of view and places us as readers pretty close to one character, known to us simply as Bourne, a private in the British Army. (It might be helpful to think of this as *third person close* point of view.)

This scene takes place just after a battle when many men have died and Bourne and the other soldiers are sleeping in the muddy holes they've dug in the walls of their trench.

> *Once during the night Bourne started up in an access of inexplicable horror, and after a moment of bewildered recollection, turned over and tried to sleep again. He remembered nothing of the nightmare which had roused him, if it were a nightmare, but gradually his awakened sense felt a vague restlessness troubling equally the other men. He noticed it first in Shem, whose body, almost touching his own, gave a quick, convulsive jump, and continued twitching for a moment, while he muttered unintelligibly, and worked his lips as though he were trying to moisten them. The obscure disquiet passed fitfully from one to another, lips parted with the sound of a bubble bursting, teeth met grinding as the jaws worked, there were little whimperings which quickened into sobs, passed into long shuddering moans, or culminated in angry, half-articulate obscenities and then relapsed, with*

fretful, uneasy movements and heavy breathing, into a more profound sleep.

Here, Manning lets us see what Bourne sees and feel what Bourne feels, but also gives us just a tiny bit of space. We aren't exactly in Bourne's head, but we might as well be sitting on his shoulder. Sometimes that closeness allows readers to easily step into the character's shoes, or in this case puttees and boots, and put themselves into the story. With that tiny bit of distance, they can easily envision themselves as that character.

These two points of view, first person singular and third person close are by far the most common. It is actually rare to find other points of view represented.

Manning stays with Bourne's point of view throughout the book, but you don't have to. Some writers will write in the voice of more than one character, shifting points of view throughout the work. It's challenging for author and reader to shift to another character's point of view. It allows readers to get differing views and to allow you as a writer to fully develop more than one character in the work. If you decide to do this, it's usually best to limit yourself to one point of view per scene. Otherwise, you're likely to confuse your reader.

William Faulkner shifts points of view quite often in his writing. His first novel *Soldier's Pay* shifts POV several times between characters, but it is in his later works, particularly *As I Lay Dying,* where he moves most gracefully between multiple characters' points of view, one of whom is a marginally functional child.

Faulkner really is a master of form and we rightly lean on him quite a bit for examples. His short story "A Rose for Emily" pulls off one of the most difficult technical points in his bag of tricks: writing in the first person plural, as if a town or a group of people are speaking to us as the narrator.

The opening line of the story is:

> *When Miss Emily Grierson died, our whole town went to her funeral: the men through a sort of respectful affection for a fallen monument, the women mostly out of curiosity to see the inside of her house, which no one save an old man-servant—a combined gardener and cook—had seen in at least ten years.*

The story continues on for 3,700 or so words, all of it presented from the first person multiple point of view, until it ends thus:

> *Then we noticed that in the second pillow was the indentation of a head. One of us lifted something from it, and leaning forward, that faint and invisible dust dry and acrid in the nostrils, we saw a long strand of iron-gray hair.*

As the story open, it doesn't seem unusual to be told the "our whole town went to her funeral." But as it ends, the narrator tells us that "we noticed" that "one of us lifted" or that "we saw a long strand of iron-gray hair." This is a unusual. It speaks to a shared experience, of course, but it also speaks to a shared sensibility. We are actually inside the head of a hydra, a multi-headed creature with individual perceptions but a single consciousness. In fact, we do not have a narrator, we have narrators—first person multiple voice. It is a rarely used technique, and this is masterful work.

Another rarely used technique is the second person point of view. In this point of view the reader receives the story from a narrator speaking directly to the reader as *you.* Italian writer, Italo Calvino's novel *If on a Winter's Night a Traveler* shifts points of view between even and odd numbered sections (it's hard to call them chapters) with the odd-numbered sections appearing in the second person. Calvino opens the first odd-numbered section thus:

You are about to begin reading Italo Calvino's new novel, If on a winter's night a traveler. Relax. Concentrate. Dispel every other thought. Let the world around you fade. Best to close the door; the TV is always on in the next room.

Reading the second person sometimes feels a lot like you're being lectured to. But it can also be a kind of a veiled "I" position where the narrator uses the point of view to create a bit of distance between his or her experience and the telling of the story.

That's worth thinking about just a little. The narrator in your story is telling the story to the reader. It will feel to the reader that the narrator is speaking directly to him or her.

This is the goal anyway. You want your reader to be completely enveloped in the story. But it's important to remember that the narrator remains a character in the story. We may be seeing the world from the protagonist's view, but it's all being relayed to us through the lens of the narrator. So we have to ask why the narrator is telling us the story. What's in it for him or her? What filters is he or she using and why?

This points us to the question of reliability in a first person singular narrator. We noted earlier that, in the Isaac Babel story, we understood that the narrator was telling us the story as he had experienced it. As a reader and, more importantly, as a writer, you really must consider why the narrator is confessing to you—that's what stories in first person really are after all, confessions that are often intensely personal and purposefully idiosyncratic. But why is this person confessing to us? What's his agenda? Can we trust him?

Perhaps the best known unreliable narrator in the American canon is Holden Caulfield in J.D. Salinger's *The Catcher in the Rye.* Salinger's gift to us is this troubled young man telling us his story. Throughout, we are confronted with Holden's inability or unwillingness to conform to societal norms. But our view of this is uniquely from Holden himself. Gradually throughout the novel, Salinger (who went ashore on D-Day with the 4th Infantry Division) peels back the onion, deftly allowing us peeks into Holden's psyche. He reveals slowly Holden's unreliability.

One terrific thing about reading an unreliable narrator story is the opportunity it offers us to fully engage with the narrator's psyche. There is a clear play between what the narrator tells us and what we discover to be the truth, so our attention is divided between what the narrator says and what we understand is happening—both within the story and within the narrator's psyche—and why.

Choosing when the reader will discover that a narrator isn't reliable is part of the joy of this technique. If you as the author decide you want to reveal it at the outset, you could have your narrator say something clearly untrue, like: *The quality of the food in Paris declined precipitously following Germany's victory in the Second World War.* Or you could have your narrator say, *"The man with the pistol said 'welcome to your new home.' I looked up and saw the sign at the gate for the first and apparently last time. It read Wyoming State Hospital for the Criminally Insane."* Either of these would be pretty good clues that your narrator might not be totally reliable.

On the other hand, you may want to savor the secret and hold the revelation back from the reader; you could wait until the denouement, sometime after the climax of the story to reveal that the narrator is somewhat untrustworthy.

Sometimes you will want to give the reader a magisterial, epic view. In this case you would use the Third Person Omniscient point of view. This view is the voice of God, or at least the voice of *a* god. It sees all, knows all and tells, well, almost all. It gives readers a real sense of what's at stake because the narrator knows things the protagonist wouldn't or couldn't know.

Tolstoy, who fought in the Crimean War, chose the Third Person Omniscient for his epic *War and Peace.*

> *One would have thought that under the almost incredibly wretched conditions the Russian soldiers were in at that time—lacking warm boots and sheepskin coats, without a roof over their heads, in the snow with eighteen degrees of frost, and without even full rations (the commissariat did not always keep up with the troops) - they would have presented a very sad and depressing spectacle.*

> *On the contrary, the army had never under the best material conditions presented a more cheerful and animated aspect. This was because all who began to grow depressed or who lost strength were sifted out of the army day by day. All the physically or morally weak had long since been left behind and only the flower of the army- physically and mentally- remained.*

> *More men collected behind the wattle fence of the Eighth Company than anywhere else. Two sergeants major were sitting with them and their campfire blazed brighter than others. For leave to sit by their wattle they demanded contributions of fuel.*

Tolstoy gives us a one-over-the-world view and magisterial tone to open this chapter: *One would have thought that under the almost incredibly wretched conditions the Russian soldiers were in at that time…* But he's also able to come down to the level of the company and the individual soldiers without breaking his point of view.

Tim O'Brien chooses this point of view in his novel *The Things They Carried*.

> *They carried all the emotional baggage of men who might die. Grief, terror, love, longing—these were intangibles, but the intangibles had their own mass and specific gravity, they had tangible weight. They carried shameful memories. They carried the common secret of cowardice barely restrained, the instinct to run or freeze or hide, and in many respects this was the heaviest burden of all, for it could never be put down, it required perfect balance and perfect posture. They carried their reputations. They carried the soldier's greatest fear, which was the fear of blushing. Men killed, and died, because they were embarrassed not to. It was what had brought them to the war in the first place, nothing positive, no dreams of glory or honor, just to avoid the blushing of dishonor. They died so as not to die of embarrassment. They crawled into tunnels and walked point and advanced under fire. Each morning, despite the unknowns, they made their legs move. They endured. The kept humping. They did not submit to the obvious alternative, which was simply to close the eyes and fall. So easy, really. Go limp and tumble to the ground and let the muscles unwind and not speak and not budge until your buddies picked you up and lifted you into the chopper that would roar and dip its nose and carry you to the world. A mere matter of falling, yet no one ever fell. It was not courage, exactly; the object was not valor. Rather, they were too frightened to be cowards.*

O'Brien's omniscient view seems a little closer to the ground. He keeps us closer by not using phrases Tolstoy throws around like *one would have thought.* But O'Brien keeps us at a distance by using the third person plural pronoun *they* and by stressing things that *men* did (*men killed, and died*) rather than what *the men* or *a man* did.

An expansive omniscient point of view, one in which the narrator informs the reader of information that the characters in the story do not have—and might wish to know—is called universal omniscient. Think of stories where the narrator might say, "little did they know...". That sort of style invites readers into the narrator's confidence, but can also seem conspiratorial—and maybe lower the expectation of reliability and trust.

Let's look at one more aspect of POV: objectivity. Obviously, the first person POV offer very limited objectivity. The first person narrator is telling us the story from his or her distinct point of view.

Within third person point of view, there is some range of objectivity. From a third person close (or limited) POV, the narrator tells us what the protagonist see, feels, knows, etc. This view is subjective.

But it is possible to have a narrator speak from a completely objective—in terms of the characters—point of view. Think of this as a documentary camera view or a fly-on-the-wall view. We only learn what we're told, not what's happening in side the characters' heads or hearts. Characters in this view must act out their feelings or explain them in a expository moment if they are to become known to the reader. In this case, the narrator cannot be a known entity to the readers, and there is no relationship between the narrator and the characters in the story.

Exercises:

1. Imagine a scene with multiple characters. Create a short scene from the point of view of each of the characters involved. Emphasize their different perspectives, desires, and agendas. Use third person close point of view.

2. Think about something that happened to you today. Invent a character experiencing a specific need or emotion and describe that scene as he or she would have experienced it using first person.

3. Pick a scene you've written earlier—even if it's one of the earlier exercises. Write it in another POV, either 1st or 3rd.

NARRATIVE STRUCTURE AND PLOT

The way a story flows, from the first words the reader sees to the last period, is the structure of the story. Many writers talk about writing a narrative as an arc, bending the story from the opening through the ups and downs of the characters' lives to its conclusion. Literary structuralists like to map out stories and diagram the narrative structure as if they were designing a house.

One of the simplest ways to think about this is to divide a story into three parts:

> —Exposition: setting up the story, telling the reader what's happening, showing what the characters want.
> —Conflict: introducing an obstacle to the characters reaching their goals.
> —Resolution: solving the problem, achieving the desire.

Here's an example: Boy meets girl and they fall in love (exposition); boy and girl learn they are members of rival family clans and are forbidden to marry (conflict); one or both of them dies (resolution). This is a slight oversimplification of a pretty well known story, but you get the idea.

Gustav Freytag was a German novelist who described narrative structure in five parts—he drew them out in a rough pyramid form— and this seems to many people to be a more accurate description of how narratives work:

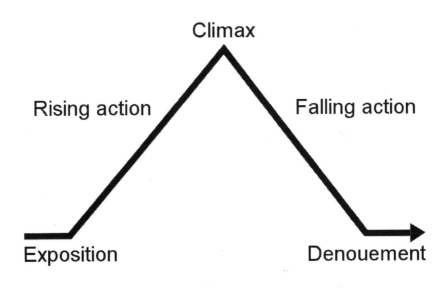

Freytag's Pyramid

In the introduction, or the first act of a five-element structure, exposition provides the background information needed to properly understand the story, such as identifying the protagonist, the antagonist, the basic conflict, and the setting. It ends with the inciting moment, which is the incident without which there would be no story. The inciting moment, a point of no return, sets the remainder of the story in motion.

In the second act, rising action provides the basic internal conflict in the story. Our hero's life is complicated by the introduction of conflicts, obstacles that frustrate the protagonist's attempt to reach his goal. Secondary conflicts can include adversaries of lesser importance than the story's antagonist, who may work with the antagonist or separately, by and for themselves or actions unknown.

The third act is that of the climax or turning point, which marks a change for the better or the worse, in the protagonist's affairs. If the story is a comedy, things will have gone badly for the protagonist up to this point; now, the tide, so to speak, will turn, and things will begin to go well for him or her. If the story is a tragedy, the opposite will ensue, with things going from good to bad or bad to worse for the protagonist.

In the fourth act, the falling action, leads us to the point of reversal: the point where the conflict unravels, with the protagonist winning or losing against the antagonist. The falling action might contain a moment of final suspense, during which the final outcome of the conflict is in doubt.

The finale, the denouement, is the point where you as the author have to tie up all the loose ends. In a comedy this is usually where the secondary characters get their come-uppance or win their prizes. In a tragedy it's where someone we care about is carried in on his shield.

The French-Bulgarian philosopher Tzvetan Todorov believes that narrative structures all involve a movement from one state of equilibrium to another by way of a state of disequilibrium. Todorov also uses a five-part structure to describe this.

> —At the outset, there is a state of equilibrium: all is good with the world.
> —An action is introduced to create a sense or state of disequilibrium.
> —The reader and characters recognize the disruption.
> —The characters act to heal the disruption.
> —A new state of equilibrium is reached.

Another model would simply divide the protagonist's world into ordinary and extraordinary. The story could chronicle a movement from the protagonist's ordinary, everyday world to an extraordinary world, following the movement from one world or the other, some variation of up and down or simply the desire to get to the ordinary—to go home. Some of my friends label the ordinary world Green World and the extraordinary Mad World. This is particularly helpful way of looking at stories if you're trying to determine a character's motivation or where the conflict in a story lies. Simply ask, what is Green World, what does this person want?

We've been going on for some time now with no real examples. That's because it's hard to demonstrate the narrative structure of a novel or a short story in a couple paragraphs. But we can do so with a poem. Yes, poems have narrative structure.

Let's look back at the Siegfried Sassoon poem we saw earlier:

Trench Duty

Shaken from sleep, and numbed and scarce awake,
Out in the trench with three hours' watch to take,
I blunder through the splashing mirk; and then
Hear the gruff muttering voices of the men
Crouching in cabins candle-chinked with light.
Hark! There's the big bombardment on our right
Rumbling and bumping; and the dark's a glare
Of flickering horror in the sectors where
We raid the Boche; men waiting, stiff and chilled,
Or crawling on their bellies through the wire.
'What? Stretcher-bearers wanted? Some one killed?'
Five minutes ago I heard a sniper fire:
Why did he do it? ... Starlight overhead—
Blank stars. I'm wide-awake; and some chap's dead.

At its core, this poem is a very short story that takes place in five acts. Let's take it apart. Here is Act I, what Freytag would call Exposition. It all happens in the first three lines:

> *Shaken from sleep, and numbed and scarce awake*
> *Out in the trench with three hours' watch to take,*
> *I blunder through the splashing mirk; and then*

Okay, so far we've learned that our protagonist, who conveniently doubles as our narrator, was asleep when we start but he is shaken awake to stand guard duty. He stumbles out in the dark into a soaked, muddy trench, and then … the line stops.

This is classic exposition. It's setting. We know it's dark and wet and we're in a trench. Our protagonist is numb; it's the middle of the night after all. He is scarcely awake. We imagine him stumbling a bit in the dark. We are fully engaged in this when we get to Act II, Rising Action.

> *Hear the gruff muttering voices of the men*
> *Crouching in cabins candle-chinked with light.*
> *Hark! There's the big bombardment on our right*

Remember, the previous line ended with "and then." This is the literary equivalent of "join us next week when we'll see if Lassie really does get Timmy out of the well. " So we're expecting something. Sassoon gives it to us he hears the men muttering—about what? They are crouching in their cabins with candles when all of a sudden Bang!, or more accurately, Hark! There's the big bombardment on our right. We're heading right into the thick of it now, just in time for Act III, Climax.

> *Rumbling and bumping; and the dark's aglare*
> *Of flickering horror in the sectors where*
> *We raid the Boche; men waiting, stiff and chilled,*

The war is on. Artillery is raining down, *rumbling and bumping*, flares are up—*the dark's aglare*. Out where they've been fighting the Germans day after day, it's a flickering horror. And through it all, the soldiers are waiting, stiff and chilled. They are anticipating the coming... what? This is the highest point of tension in the poem. It comes just before things begin to come to resolution in Act IV, Falling Action.

> *Or crawling on their bellies through the wire.*
> *What? Stretcher-bearers wanted? Someone killed?'*

In this little two-line snippet, we learn that there is more than just the artillery falling. Some of our comrades are outside the trench, crawling through the wire. The flares, we remember are up, it's raining artillery off on our right and these poor guys are crawling in the mud back to our lines. Suddenly we learn that someone is dead. We've reached resolution. In this case, death. Now, Act V, Denouement.

> *Five minutes ago I heard a sniper fire:*
> *Why did he do it? ... Starlight overhead—*
> *Blank stars. I'm wide-awake; and some chap's dead.*

We can imagine two soldiers talking *sotto voce* at one edge of the trench so that others won't hear. We're back alone with the protagonist and his thoughts, little images remaining to ground us before the conclusion: *I'm wide awake and some chap's dead.*

This short narrative poem tells a little story and we can break it out into five distinct acts. It's worth pointing out that the climax of the work isn't necessarily when the most important thing happens—it's the moment just before, when the tension is the greatest. That moment, the look into the maw of what is to come, leads us to Act IV or the falling action, when things begin to roll towards resolution. Think of it as the point at the very top of the roller coaster, just before you tip over the edge.

We've looked at the architecture of stories, how stories are built. But now we have to decide how to put the words in place, how to tell the story itself. This is the plot. It is the sequence of events in your story, how they relate and how the order in which you present them. Even if you know how the major events should fall in the story—the rise of action from exposition to climax to denouement, you have to decide how to tell the story itself.

One way is simply to start at the beginning and tell it straight through in chronological order. Ernst Junger's masterpiece memoir *Storm of Steel* works this way. It opens with his first day at the front, his first day of war, and proceeds in a rather straight line through his many battles, wounds, promotions and awards, and ultimately his disillusionment and the defeat of the German army. This is a linear story structure.

Another way to tell the story is to open the story at a convenient spot and then jump backward or forward in time as needed to tell the story to best effect. This is a modular story structure. Kurt Vonnegut's novel-in-the-form-of-a-memoir-cum-science-fiction-fantasy, *Slaughterhouse-Five* does this, beginning with the narrator, speaking from a point in time well after the events that make up the body of the story, saying, "*All this happened, more or less.*" The story then jumps around in time going off in some rather bizarre and wonderful directions with protagonist Billy Pilgrim being captured at the Battle of the Bulge and interned at the POW camp called Slaughterhouse Five, the firebombing of Dresden, an actress named Montana Wildhack, and aliens from the planet Tralfalmadore.

My point in choosing these two wildly disparate works as examples is to show that plot matters as much in non-fiction as in fiction. If you're writing a novel, a memoir, or even if you're writing your story just to leave for your grandkids, plot—the way you sequence the events, the cause and effects of the action in your story—matters.

Some people believe there are only two kinds of plotlines:

—A stranger comes to town
—Someone goes on a voyage of discovery

I think this is rather too simplistic. But it illustrates an important element of writing and maybe of life: There is always another way of seeing things. These really are the same stories from a different point of view: The person who goes on the voyage *is* the stranger coming to town.

We'll look at different types of plots in a little while, but let's first figure out what makes a plot. To begin with, it should have at least three elements: a beginning, a middle and an end. It should also have some clear cause and effect. But most importantly, it needs some source of tension, of conflict.

Let's look at Michener's *Tales from the South Pacific* again: *Ensign Nellie Forbush got married* isn't a plot; it's an event. *Ensign Nellie Forbush overcame her racist upbringing and married the man she loved, a French expatriate planter with two mixed-race children, who also happens to be a murderer*, is a plot.

Conflict makes the plot. Nellie has desires—to marry Emile de Becque—but the author has put some obstacles in her way: Nellie happens to be a racist. Oh, she wouldn't think of herself as a racist, that's just way things are in Little Rock, Arkansas in 1942, she would say. But she is a racist and since Emile has these two children that he fathered with a dark-skinned native woman, now deceased, this is a problem, an obstacle for Nellie. That Nellie overcomes her racism is the story. How Michener puts the story together is the plot.

There are different types or models of plots. The Nellie Forbush story is told as partially a coming-of-age story and part peeling-back-the-onion story. I'll explain.

A coming-of-age story is one in which the protagonist grows up in the midst of the story. Specifically, we're talking about emotional and moral growth. The protagonist will come of age emotionally during the novel. Any novel needs character development, but a coming-age-story (the technical term of art here is *Bildungsroman*: German for formation novel) exists solely as the story of this change. One of the best-known American coming-of-age novels is D-Day and Battle of the Bulge veteran J.D. Salinger's iconic *The Catcher in the Rye*.

A peeling-back-the-onion story is one in which we, the readers, learn a little bit more about the characters at each turn in the story. Faulkner is the great master of this type of story and his novel *Absolom, Absolom!* is one of the best because, as usual, Faulkner gives us different voices telling the story and has each voice reveal a slightly deeper and slightly different element of the plot.

These are archetypal story lines or plotlines. There are other archetypes as well. Several plot types are structured around some element of time. One could be called the Ticking Clock. In a story like this, the protagonist is usually fighting a clock. If he or she doesn't complete some task within a certain time, something dire will occur. A variation of this is an 11th Hour story. In this model, time is already running short when we join the story. Another classic model is called a Day-in-the-Life story. Just as it is described, this is the story of a single day in the life of the protagonist. In a Big Bang story, plots like the 11th Hour story or the Ticking Clock story are turned around: Something dramatic happens and the story takes off from there. A Blue Moon story is one that takes place around a rare but recurring event—werewolf stories might fall into this category.

There are forms that highlight relationships. A Sidekick story is one told from the point of view of someone very close to the protagonist. A Buddy story focuses on the relationship between two generally equal and often unlikely partners and their exploits. Gathering stories are usually done with ensemble casts and bring together groups for weddings, funerals, reunions and so forth. The tension here is often some conflict long suppressed or some revelation during the event.

There are of course combinations of these archetypal stories, too. A British World War I veteran wrote a pretty well-known coming-of-age-sidekick-voyage-11th Hour story called *The Lord of the Rings*. J.R.R. Tolkien also fought at the Somme.

Everything we've seen so far seems to point towards conflict as a principal driver in plot. Conflict defines your characters and gives them reason to act. So let's lay out some different types of conflict that you might use in your story.

We'll shoot the close-in targets first: internal conflict, a person at war with him or herself. Internal conflict is something internal that pulls or pushed your characters to act or fail to act. Your fear of dying in a hail of gunfire playing out against your buddy's cries for help as he lies wounded in the kill zone. That's a pretty serious and obvious internal conflict.

Very often we see two people in conflict with each other. This is inter-personal conflict. It can be direct combat or, more subtly, a parent and a teenage son or daughter.

There can be a person in conflict against nature—the violent storm in Lawrence's memoir we looked at earlier fits this.

The more subtle and difficult conflicts to pull off include a person struggling against society and person struggling against fate. You could say that a person in conflict against society might be a person in conflict against the society they've chosen—like the military. So perhaps this could be a story where someone isn't accepted into his unit or ship's crew until some dramatic action occurs.

What's important about conflict is that it tends to shape the protagonist as well as the story, often dynamically and sometimes dramatically. Although it's sometimes unbelievable to see people so dramatically changed by a conflict that they begin to act in ways that are antithetical to their previous nature, like a Klansman whose worldview is so altered by some event that he rushes out and marries a black woman. It is nonetheless one of the principle and necessary elements of story telling. As a writer you use it for specific purposes, including shaping the story and keeping your readers' attention. But you also use it to give yourself time to do some other things. Ratcheting up tension keeps the reader engaged and wanting to turn pages. This allows you the time to do some work on character, theme and description. See how all of this is starting to come together?

Exercises.

1. Tell the story of your day and relate it chronologically, beginning with the introduction of some element of tension and keep the tension escalating. Once you've completed this, determine what's left to add: background, context, texture?

2. Chose three events at random—say a traffic jam, a picked pocket, running into an old acquaintance on the street. Write them in various sequences, emphasizing the way or ways in which one event builds on the previous.

THEME

Sooner or later, someone will ask you, "What is your book about?" If you're lucky, this will happen sooner and the person will be a friend. If someone asks you early enough, it might save you a lot of time and heartache.

This seems like an easy question. "My book is about the war in Afghanistan" or "My book is about my time as a drill sergeant," would be appropriate answers. But they would be incomplete. The plot of your book might involve the war in Afghanistan or your time on the trail, but the theme of your book—what your book is really about—is something altogether different.

The theme of a book or a story, whether it's fiction or non-fiction, is the principal idea you the author are trying to get across to the reader. It is the real reason you're writing the story in the first place: You have something worth saying about the human experience. The story is the vehicle you use to expose what you want to say about the human condition, the theme.

Tobias Wolff's short story "Coming Attractions" takes place in hedonistic 1970s California. The protagonist is a teenage girl, Jean, who works at the local movie theater. Her boss has taken off to go ice skating, leaving Jean to close up. He's expected back any minute to lock the doors and give her a ride home. But he's late. So, in a world without the internet or other distractions, Jean picks up the telephone and starts calling people.

First, she calls people she knows: her mother, who isn't at home but rather out on a date with "Uncle Nick"; her father, whose new wife answers and brushes Jean off without letting her speak to her dad; a random guy she finds in the phone book, Mr. Love. Finally, Jean's boss, Mr. Munson, comes in. He has a freshly broken his ankle and is on crutches. He tosses Jean a five-dollar bill and tells her to take a cab home. The story continues, and I haven't really done justice to Wolff's story, but you can see the way things are trending: All of the adults in Jean's life are kind of absent. They are all narcissists, turned completely inside themselves and unable to provide Jean with what she desperately needs: adult leadership, a role model.

Wolff's story is ostensibly about a young California girl who often has to do things for herself and sometimes gets into trouble. But it is about much more than that. At the story's end, Jean has dived into the pool at her apartment to drag a red bicycle out of the deep end for her little brother, Tucker. She has stepped up and taken action to provide for someone she views as being in her charge. So, the moral of the story might be that the narcissism and absence of adults around Jean aren't necessarily deadly. She steps up and accepts her evolving role, her coming adulthood, and they all presumably survive. So perhaps one theme of "Coming Attractions" is that even without perfect adults in our lives, we usually turn out okay.

Let's look at a longer work: James Jones' novel *From Here to Eternity*. This is a book about life in the military. It takes place in Hawaii on the eve of Pearl Harbor. The soldiers in the story lead individually desperate, but workaday, peacetime army lives. Leaders are more focused on winning the division boxing title than on building a combat ready force. Soldiers struggle to find their proper place in the army and the world. People drink and fight and cheat on their spouses.

We could spend pages describing the plot of *From Here to Eternity*, but that might discourage you from reading the book. It is worth the read. Suffice it to say that all the major characters at one point or another face a dilemma involving a force or fate larger than themselves. Throughout the book and its two sequels (*The Thin Red Line* and *Whistle*), Jones pits men and women against immovable or immutable forces—the army, love and a World War among them. Man's problems are puny bantams, small and irrelevant, when viewed against a force of nature or against a world at war. This is the theme.

Important tip: Notice that Jones doesn't solve the problem. The object isn't to show how to overcome these forces. It is simply to illuminate them and their power over measly little men and women. Philosophers might feel the need to solve the world's problems. We are merely writers. Our job is to expose them honestly.

But how do we do that? One thing to keep in mind is that you might not know what your story is really about when you start writing. Maybe you want to just sit down and write a story about an American sailor fighting a ground war in a land-locked desert country. That could be interesting. Maybe the sailor joined the military to get a job skill and access to college money. He became a corpsman and was assigned to Fleet Marine Force. Now that sailor, who really wanted only to get some money for college and maybe become a physician's assistant, is looking at a Marine lying wounded in the middle of a dusty street after being shot in a firefight. The bullets are still flying and the Marine is calling for help. Now this could be really interesting when the corpsman has to decide whether or not to rush out into the kill zone and rescue the guy. Especially if the wounded Marine had looked down on the corpsman and ridiculed him for joining the Navy rather than Marine Corps. Now there's a story that addresses themes like: All actions have unpredictable consequences, challenges to personal courage, questions of integrity and honor, or maybe facing down a bully.

There are some more or less universal themes: man's struggle against society or man's struggle against man; coming of age, initiation into a group; Carpe Diem; and whether fate can defeat all of man's efforts to make the future his own or whether he is free to choose his own path. There are more, of course.

Which of these or other themes might describe your story? A story about basic training could very easily be a story about rites of initiation—basic is all about transformation from civilian to soldier—or about coming of age. A story about a young airman who doesn't do well in garrison but excels in combat could be a story about man's struggle against society. Now you just have to sort out where in your story the theme lies.

Let's look at another Siegfried Sassoon poem.

When you are standing at your hero's grave,
Or near some homeless village where he died,
Remember, through your heart's rekindling pride,
The German soldiers who were loyal and brave.
Men fought like brutes; and hideous things were done;
And you have nourished hatred harsh and blind.
But in that Golgotha perhaps you'll find
The mothers of the men who killed your son.

I won't give you the title yet, because it's too revealing. But what do we think this poem is about? What is Sassoon's theme? First, I suppose we should ask whom the narrator is addressing. The opening line is pretty clear: *When you are standing at your hero's grave.* He's speaking to someone post-war who has come to pay respects to a fallen soldier. Sassoon writes of pride but a moment later of a mindfulness of the enemy's courage and loyalty, the very things of which the "you" being addressed by the narrator might be proud.

He reminds us all of the horrors of the war, men fighting like brutes and doing hideous things. And in the aftermath, the survivors nourish a blind, harsh hatred. But in that Golgotha (the place where Christ was crucified, a place of great pain and sacrifice) you might meet someone just like yourself, another survivor, the mother of the soldier who killed your son. Left unsaid, or unasked, is "what will you do if you meet?"

At this point, it seems to me the theme might be something like forgiveness or letting go hatred and moving on. It might be something like everyone suffers in war, every soldier at the front and all the families at home on both sides. Sassoon titled this poem "Reconciliation." I think that's his theme, that after the shared suffering, both sides, perhaps led by the mothers rather than by the diplomats and politicians, must reconcile.

There are many other points worth discussing in Sassoon's poem. We'll take two; both involve conflict. We discuss conflict in numerous places in this book and rightly so. It is often the principal driver of plot, of change in characters, of action. At the end of the first stanza Sassoon creates tension—this is conflict— by challenging the belief structure of the "you" who is addressed. "You" have come to proudly stand at the grave of your hero who died in some homeless village, (homeless and village are great in opposition to each other as well) when he reminds you that the Germans were loyal and brave. At the end of the second stanza he reminds you that they had mothers, too.

During the war it was considered necessary to dehumanize the enemy. The Germans were called "the Hun" or "the Boche" in order to instill the idea of them being a primitive, tribal people and minimize the idea of them being Europeans, people like the French and the British, so that young Englishmen would have no scruples about killing them. The Hun is bad. He is wrong. They are evil.

Sassoon voids that notion. He places the German troops on equal footing with the English who are good, who are heroes. Good versus evil or right versus wrong is too simple a vehicle to carry Sassoon's message. He humanizes the enemy and makes the work much more compelling by setting right vs. right.

Finally, Sassoon has made the Great War personal. It's easy to set two ideologies against each other, but like a story about a mountain or the wind, it's not very interesting until it becomes personal, human. Sassoon pits a human, your hero, your son, against the German soldiers who during the war displayed many of the same attributes you admire and honor. Then he takes it a step further, while you are visiting your son's grave, you might meet the mothers of the soldiers who killed him. This is intensely personal. It brings the vague notions of war and brutality down to the fact that both ideologies, both peoples, pitted young men against one another and both sides suffered at an intensely personal level. Sassoon has perfectly shaped his work to support his theme.

In the poem, Golgotha alludes to something Sassoon assumed all his readers would understand: a place of great suffering and sacrifice. An allusion is a link the author provides the reader to another piece of knowledge in hope of illuminating some point in the original piece. Sassoon is safe in using the term Golgotha because in his time a religious reference like this would be widely understood. He runs little risk of alienating his readers by referencing works of literature or mythology or pieces of art they wouldn't understand. It is also, in this case, quite economical for Sassoon; it saves space and time because he now doesn't have to say "in this place of great suffering and sacrifice."

But economy is only one reason for developing allusion. Allusions help bring your reader further into your world in a number of ways. First, you help the reader understand how you arrived at the place in your work by giving them points of reference. Further, you challenge your reader by demanding that he or she take the leap of faith necessary to make the connection.

You also take some risks when you use allusion. What if your reader doesn't make the connection? In that case maybe you've lost them. But in the modern age, with the Internet connections allowing instant searches, it's not hard to go find something.

Now let's try to link allusion to theme. For two quick examples, again we lean on Faulkner. First, the title of *As I Lay Dying* is an allusion to Homer's *Odyssey*. When Agamemnon's ghost visits Ulysses and recounts his death, he says that:

> *"As I lay dying, the woman with the dog's eyes would not close my eyes, even as I descended into hell."*

That shows us the direct connection to Homer. But how does it support Faulkner's theme? One theme in *As I Lay Dying* is duty. The novel is built around a family moving the body of their matriarch to a graveyard just after she dies. The trip is dangerous, the family faces threats from nature and man. But it is nonetheless a duty the family has accepted in accordance with Addie's wishes. There is no clear link between the allusion and this theme unless you think Clytemnestra has a duty to close Agamemnon's eyes. That's a stretch.

Another theme in the novel is one of isolation. Each part of the novel is told in first person but from the point of view of numerous characters—Darl, Dewey Dell, Jewel, Vardaman, and so on. Each person speaks from their individual point of view but full of observations about the others and often about a failure to understand or be able to influence the other. Similarly, As Agamemnon is dying, he is alone and incapable of action, he is forced to observe Clytemnestra's actions and to watch his own descent into hell. This seems to work, but only slightly better.

In the end, I think the novel's structure sets up a theme in itself, that this journey we're all on, life, is a journey of little consequence since we're all just going got end up in the dirt anyway. Faulkner places any number of obstacles in the way of the family's journey to Jefferson including a river which symbolizes the river Styx. Addie, despite the fact that she is dead, speaks to us the readers, but only after she has crossed the river (and symbolically entered hell.) So, perhaps, the title of the story is a signpost, an allusion, to the idea that we are all on the road to hell.

Faulkner's work is rife with allusion to biblical stories and mythology, but also to Shakespeare. He is sometimes subtle in his allusions, but often, just like in *As I Lay Dying*, he puts it right out in front (as the title). *The Sound and The Fury* is a direct allusion to Macbeth (Act V, scene 5) when Macbeth says: *

> *Tomorrow and tomorrow and tomorrow,*
> *Creeps in this petty pace from day to day*
> *To the last syllable of recorded time,*
> *And all our yesterdays have lighted fools*
> *The way to dusty death.*
> *Out, out, brief candle!*
> *Life's but a walking shadow, a poor player*
> *That struts and frets his hour upon the stage*
> *And then is heard no more: it is a tale*
> *Told by an idiot, full of sound and fury,*
> *Signifying nothing.*

This allusion supports Faulkner's themes perfectly. The book opens in the point of view of Benjy, a mentally retarded child—in the language of Shakespeare, perhaps, an idiot. One of the recurring themes in all of Faulkner's works is the decadence of Southern culture and the decline of Southern gentility, perhaps here represented by "*the way to dusty death.*" Finally, the significance of the past, of history, in the lives of Southerners is a dominant theme to Faulkner. He once said, "The past is not dead. It isn't even really past." The reference here to yesterdays lighting the way to dusty death highlights the folly of living on past glories.

These are relatively simple allusions. They use the same language, in some cases word for word, as the piece they allude to, and the pieces are well known. It's more difficult for us to catch—and this is the point to learn as a writer—the less obvious allusion. You have to work for it and so will your readers. Think back to our discussion of metaphor. We're touching on almost the same idea here: The writer places one thing alongside another in order to compare the two. But in the case of allusion, a writer only points to another work of art (or literature or theater or film or music) in order to help us understand something in his or her own work.

Exercises.

1. This is primarily a reading exercise. Pick a short story and read it through. Once you're done, sum up the theme of the story in one or two words. Do this with several stories over the period of a week.

2. Next, go back to each of the stories you read and read them again. Pick out actions, plot points, dialogue, or other elements of craft that point to the theme. Do this for all the stories you read.

3. Write a couple paragraphs in which a character starts a new job or returns from school at the end of the semester or is driving through a town but doesn't know where he or she is going. Once you're done think about three possible themes that could be developed from the paragraphs. What is happening in these paragraphs//scenes that point you towards a theme?

I said in the first chapter that all the examples used in the book were from books written by veterans. Shakespeare was not a soldier, but we're only using this snippet here to show the sourcing of Faulkner's allusions. Faulkner chose Shakespeare, so we need to source it to explain the allusions.

BEGINNINGS AND ENDINGS

The first sentence is the hardest. This is a truism among writers that is supposed to give one hope that the writing gets easier the further you get into your work. I'm not sure it's accurate. I do agree that simply knowing where to start a story is one of the hardest decisions you'll make.

You could start at the very beginning. You could jump in somewhere in the middle. You could start at the most important scene or event. You could even start at the end. All of these are valid options and any of them might be the right place for your story to start.

A good opening has several tasks: It *must* establish setting, tone, and point of view; it *should* establish some sense of conflict as well. Word choice, phrasing, and syntax all help the author create tone. Shorter, Germanic words with hard consonants in paragraphs with mixed sentence lengths speed the reader along into the work.

Ford Madox Ford, whom we met earlier, opens his first, and arguably most important novel, *The Good Soldier*, thus:

This is the saddest story I have ever heard.

Well, okay. We may safely assume this isn't a comedy. But is it intriguing enough to make you want to keep reading? I hope so, because it's a good read. But how does it work as an opening? Our narrator is speaking to us directly in a personal, almost conversational, way and tells us that we are going to hear a sad story. It really can't do much more than that. Nonetheless, it works well because it nearly demands that the reader move on.

We mentioned Vonnegut's opening to *Slaughterhouse-Five* earlier:

All of this happened, more or less.

We're in the same territory as with Ford. I don't mean that this one sentence comprises the entire opening of their novels. It's just to point out that the first few words are really very important to catch the reader's attention.

Here is an example of a writer giving the reader some context at the front:

On the 15th of May, 1796, General Bonaparte made his entry into Milan at the head of that young army which had shortly before crossed the Bridge of Lodi and taught the world that after all these centuries Caesar and Alexander had a successor. The miracles of gallantry and genius of which Italy was a witness in the space of a few months aroused a slumbering people; only a week before the arrival of the French, the Milanese still regarded them as a mere rabble of brigands, accustomed invariably to flee before the troops of His Imperial and Royal Majesty; so much at least was reported to them three times weekly by a little news-sheet no bigger than one's hand, and printed on soiled paper.

This is the opening of Stendhal's *The Charterhouse of Parma*. It reads a little like history, but it is a novel. Stendhal's (Marie-

Henri Beyle) novel was groundbreaking in that it included some of the first realistic depictions of battle written in novel form by a combat veteran. But let's see what he does in these few sentences that sets up the rest of the story. First, he gives us time and place. It takes him less than fifteen words to tell us where we are and when. He describes action: Napoleon, the new Caesar or Alexander the Great, enters Milan. Then he gives us some context: The Milanese are shocked to learn that Napoleon's army is so good because their government has been lying to them. This opening does what it is supposed to do; it serves mainly as an introduction to scene and setting, but it also gives us the author's tone—how he addresses the work. Stendhal's middle diction lets us know this won't be a dreary read. He moves us through a lifetime in just under 500 pages, but it doesn't lag.

But it doesn't place us into a scene. Sometimes, to really get your readers' attention, you can just open up by introducing a scene. Frederick Forsyth's opening to *The Dogs of War* does this:

> *There were no stars that night on the bush airstrip, nor any moon; just the West African darkness wrapping around the scattered groups like wet velvet. The cloud cover was lying hardly off the tops of the iroko trees, and the waiting men prayed it would stay a while longer to shield them from the bombers.*

It's night on a West African bush airstrip and men are praying the clouds will protect them from bombers. Yep, I think I'll stick around to see what happens next. Forsyth opens with short, crisp Germanic words. No description at all until the last couple words of the opening—*like wet velvet.* Notice how many hard consonants he uses. This type of writing draws the reader in and keeps their attention. It doesn't require much of the reader and doesn't send his or her mind racing off to make sense of your allusions. It just works.

Forsyth is a great opener. His opening to *Day of the Jackal* is nearly perfect in every way:

It is cold at 6:40 in the morning on a March day in Paris, and seems even colder when a man is about to be executed by firing squad. At that hour on March 11, 1963, in the main courtyard of Fort d'Ivry a French Air Force colonel stood before a stake driven into the chilly gravel as his hands were bound behind the post, and stared with slowly diminishing disbelief at the squad of soldiers facing him 20 metres away.

A foot scuffed the grit, a tiny release from tension, as the blindfold was wrapped around the eyes of Lieutenant-Colonel Jean-Marie Bastien-Thiry, age 35, blotting out the light for the last time. The mumbling of the priest was a helpless counterpoint to the crackling of twenty rifle bolts as the soldiers charged and cocked their carbines.

Beyond the walls a Berliet truck blared for a passage as a smaller vehicle crossed its path towards the centre of the city; the sound died away masking the "Take your aim" order from the officer in charge of the squad. The crash of rifle fire, when it came, caused no ripple on the waking city other than to send a flutter of pigeons skyward for a few moments. The single "whack" seconds later of the coup-de-grace was lost in the rising din of traffic from beyond the walls.

As history, Forsyth gets a detail wrong: Bastien-Thiry refused the blindfold that day. But as an opening for a novel, it is brilliant. The crispness of the words matches the chill in the air. Bastien-Thiry stares with *slowly diminishing disbelief* at the firing squad 20 metres away. Forsyth builds tension and then offers *a tiny release* to start the second paragraph. By the third paragraph we get a flash of life going on outside the scene he has set and the noise of that life sets a counterpoint to the sound of the rifle fire. Forsyth perfectly uses a French phrase, *coup de grace*, in its original usage—the single bullet administered to kill the prisoner if the firing squad fails to do so.

Let's look at some non-fiction now. American historian Ted Morgan served in the French Army during its counter insurgency in Algeria. (Morgan is a dual citizen and wrote in France as Sanche de Gramont, although his full birth name and title are: Comte St. Charles Armand Gabriel de Granmont.) His memoir of that period is called *My Battle of Algiers*. It starts like this:

> *I should explain that I got into Yale thanks to affirmative action, then known as a little help from a wealthy alumnus. In 1952, I was wasting away at the Sorbonne, at a time when France was still hungover from the Second World War. Professors advised students not to attend their overcrowded classes but to pick up mimeographed copies of their lectures. A friend of mine who was attending law school told me that on the first day of class, the dean announced to the assembled students: "Half of you will flunk out. What France needs are good carpenters, not bad lawyers."*

There are a couple lessons here. Morgan uses first person—it is a memoir after all—and makes it sound as if he is simply conversing with you, the reader. *I should explain*, he says. It's very conversational. It gives the reader a good feeling about the narrator: 'We're friends and I'm just here telling you a story.' Then he sets two conflicting images in front of you: France, still hungover from the war, and what we all (presumably) know America was like—vibrant, booming, and churning out new college graduates by the thousands thanks to the GI Bill of Rights. He sets himself (again, it is a memoir) at the center of all this: He was wasting away at the Sorbonne. He gets into Yale but needs help. But he deftly balances the uniquely individual with the universal and frames it all in terms of conflicts—the war, of course, the conflict between the students' expectations and the reality of post-war France (*what France needs...*), and the differences between France and the United States.

But what's really interesting about what Morgan does here is this: He uses this opening paragraph as a type of metaphor for his life. Ted Morgan is an anagram for De Gramont. Morgan's life is split between France and America, between being French and being American, between being Ted Morgan and being De Gramont. So he shows us this division in the very first paragraph of his memoir by showing us the differences between France and the United States and between his life in one versus the other. This is masterful.

We need to digress just a bit to talk about the memoir form. Unlike an autobiography, which covers the entire lifespan of the author, a memoir is a book written to cover a specific period of the author's life during which, we hope, something momentous happened. The author takes this momentous time or event and draws a lesson for the rest of us. For example, Tobias Wolff has written two memoirs: *A Boy's Life* and *In Pharaoh's Army*. They cover his childhood and his service in the army in Vietnam.

Many service members write memoirs, others churn out novels about their service or the war, lightly camouflaging the characters. Regardless, this is right in the wheelhouse for military writers and whether you choose fiction or non-fiction is a personal decision. Here are a few things to think about.

—If you're going to write non-fiction, tell the truth. We mentioned this earlier, but it bears repeating. This means that you're going to expose events and actions that might be sensitive to others. You don't need their permission to write about them, but you do owe them the dignity of truthfulness.

—If you are writing for publication, remember that your friends and family might prefer to not appear in your work.

Especially if they appear in a less than flattering light. This could be the fast lane to losing friends and alienating family.

—Some of the events you want to write about might expose information that is sensitive to the military, especially in wartime. Think about what you have to say and how it could be either misconstrued or in some other way used as a weapon against your comrades-in-arms or your country.

—This goes double for secrets with the added danger of prison for releasing classified material.

—Ask yourself when you want to write and publish. Sometimes your perspective increases with distance and time.

—There is a trend in literature these days of authors writing autobiographical novels or fictionalized memoirs. By all means consider these hybrid forms, but think clearly about what you want to say and why. Hybrid forms are successfully managed only by very highly competent literary writers.

Now, about endings. We discussed the narrative arc of stories earlier and noted that the highest point of the story—the climax—doesn't come at the end. The end of the story is where, after the climax and denouement, the author ties up all the loose ends, making sure that any unresolved plotlines are closed. We can talk a bit about forms here, too.

A short story is a piece of fiction where (usually) one significant event occurs. The event can trigger action by the protagonist or action against the protagonist. Short stories are usually somewhere around 5,000 words, but can vary. Anything reaching the 10,000-word point is probably a novelette or a novella, and a novel usually checks in at over 40,000 words.

In non-fiction, essays can run from 1,000 words to 5,000 and beyond; long-form journalism can reach 10,000 words easily. Beyond these lengths, you might end up serializing your work or finding that it really has become a book-length work. This book contains about 41,000 words.

In a short story or shorter essay you probably won't have too many loose ends to tie up. But as you spread out into longer forms, it's easy to leave loose ends. Your readers will most assuredly notice if they get to the end of the book and one of their favorite characters is missing or fails to get his or her comeuppance. So you have to remember all the twists and turns and tangles you create in the story, and make sure you close them all off by the end.

But the end is also where you have to make sure that your reader has had sufficient opportunity to get the point of your story. You have to make sure that your reader is rewarded for sticking with you through the work. We talked about theme earlier. Let's re-visit it here. The thing you're writing about, the big point you're trying to convey is the theme of the work. If you've been tricky about it, if you've obscured the theme of the work in some way, the end is where you have to come clean. Your reader wants to know what you're trying to tell him or her. If you fail at this, your readers might close the book and be confused. It's your failure, not theirs.

Some writers like to close their works by returning to the opening—a circular ending. In a journey or coming of age story this is a somewhat predictable ending: The sailor goes on a voyage around the world and returns home triumphant. A well-known example of this is, again, J.R.R. Tolkien's *Lord of the Rings* trilogy: The first book opens in the Shire and the final book brings Frodo and Sam back to the Shire to end the War of the Ring.

Other writers work to create a surprise ending, sometimes called a trick ending. Perhaps the best-known trick/surprise ending is Ambrose Bierce's *An Occurrence at Owl Creek Bridge*. Bierce, who fought in many Civil War battles, fools us throughout the middle of the story and only brings us back to reality in the last full paragraph with "a stunning blow upon the back of the neck." The trick isn't really in the ending; it's in the middle. But the ending is certainly a surprise.

Generations ago, most endings were simply epilogues: the place in the story where the marriage or death we've been anticipating occurs, or where just rewards are distributed—where the protagonist gets the girl and the antagonist gets the shaft.

This began to change in the late 19th and early 20th centuries. Writers began to play with endings to make the entire story more interesting.

Some began to write what could be called reverse epilogues. One way to do this is to rely on a series of flashbacks beginning just after the opening. Instead of showing what happens to the characters as a result of the events of the story, the author shows what happened to the characters to get them to the point where the story began.

Stories don't always need to end neatly. Some stories just seem to stop, while others have conflicting events or multiple endings. These might be called open or ambiguous endings. John Fowles's *The French Lieutenant's Woman* is one of these. Fowles actually gives the reader three endings. An uncertain or ambiguous ending—kind of an anti-epilogue—leaves the reader wondering what happens or allows the reader to concoct an ending that pleases them.

Writers whose narrators aren't particularly savvy can have endings that leave the characters in one place and the readers in another. If a character doesn't understand what has happened to him or her, or doesn't evolve in an expected way throughout the course of the story, the reader winds up with a different understanding of the story than the characters. This externalizes the events, particularly the climax, in a way that often allows the reader to learn a great deal about the characters even while the characters don't seem to have figured out what happened or why.

Why would you use each of these endings? Your choice of how to end a story might be part of your theme. If you are writing about decisions and consequences but your point is that things don't always turn out how one expects them to, you could get a kicker at the end by leaving events unresolved. If your theme is about the importance of place, then a circular ending to a journey story makes a great deal of sense.

Or if you simply want to show that regardless of our puny human actions the world continues to turn a story without a clear end—one that simply stops—might help reinforce your point. A trick or surprise ending is used simply to surprise the reader. Take the reader to a place where their expectations are clearly moving in one direction, then jerk the rug out from under them with a twist. The point is that how you structure your story—how it opens and closes especially—should support your theme.

A note about suspense and surprise. We discussed trick endings as jerking the rug out from under your reader. This can be done successfully and it can fail miserably. You nearly always want to create suspense in your work; it shouldn't be evident on page 25 where a story is going to be on page 250. That said, the way your characters and your plot behave can be suspenseful without being too surprising. A little surprise goes a long way, but the value of it to your reader wears off quickly. Suspense, however, can build and build until your reader needs to feel the release from the tension.

Finally, the ending of a novel should likely dramatize a defining moment for your characters, particularly if it is a life story. Often the ending of a novel is revelatory—some great epiphany for the reader and the protagonist occurs. This summarizes the story, puts a coda at the end for the reader. But there might also be something pointing ahead. Ending with something like, "But Hallie felt her belly and knew something even bigger was coming," presages more to follow.

Exercises:

1. Write an opening to a story involving three people, one of whom is passing judgment on another who does not speak the judge's language. The third person is the interpreter. This can be from any of the characters' point of view but should be in the past tense.

2. Now write the same scene in any tense or point of view you want, but make it the closing paragraphs of the story.

3. Write the ending paragraph of a story that provides the reader with a hint that something will come later that neither of the two main characters could ever predict. Could you turn that paragraph into an opening paragraph? Try it.

DIALOGUE

Now that you've built the setting and determined the point of view, decided on the theme and plot, and set your characters to motion, it's time to have your characters start talking to one another. There is probably nothing harder or more important than putting words in your characters' mouths. This is how your characters reveal themselves, it is how your plot unfolds, it is the core of your work whether fiction or non-fiction.

You could think about dialogue as falling into three broad categories: expository, responsive, and non-responsive.

Expository language is used by the author principally to tell rather than show. It gets a terribly bad rap from writers, but is sometimes a necessary element. If it is done well, no one can complain. If it's done poorly, everyone will. Writers, especially screenwriters, like to joke about how badly this can be done. The joke line is typically something like, "As you know, your father, the King....." This is bad expository writing.

Ian Fleming does expository dialogue pretty well. Fleming, of course, wrote the James Bond spy novels, and he always has the villain explain his plot to Bond just before he sends Bond off, ostensibly to his death. This is from Dr. No:

"Ah, yes. You must have been wondering, Mister Bond. You have the habit of inquiry. It persists even to the last, even into the shadows. I admire such qualities in a man with only a few hours to live. So I will tell you. I will turn over the next page. It will console you. There is more to this place than bird dung. Your instincts did not betray you."

Doctor No paused for emphasis. 'This island, Mister Bond, is about to be developed into the most valuable technical intelligence centre in the world."

"Really?' Bond kept his eyes bent on his hands.

"Doubtless you know that Turks Island, about three hundred miles from here through the Windward Passage, is the most important centre for testing the guided missiles of the United States?"

Fleming has Dr. No reveal—or *expose*—his plan to Bond rather than having Bond uncover it through action. This is neither good nor bad, it's Fleming's technique; it's his shtick, he does it in every one of his novels.

Responsive dialogue is when two people are actually engaging in a conversation, responding to each others' cues.

"So when did you get back from Norfolk?" Helen asked.

"About two weeks ago," Peter said.

"Huh, and it took you this long to stop in?"

"Yeah, I was really busy with getting the apartment squared away."

"Really? It has one room. What could possibly take so long?"

You see the flow of the conversation. There may or may not be something else happening in this scene, but it plays as a simple question-and-answer series. Helen asks a question and Peter replies and so on.

In non-responsive dialogue, the speakers don't respond directly, there is often something else going on in the conversation and each character has an individual objective to the conversation.

"Just tell me what you want to do about it," she said.

"Look, I have to go soon. So we don't have much time" He was getting tipsy.

"What's the difference, anyway? Alice isn't going to be there."

"I'll figure it out once I'm there. Can you mange by yourself for the week?"

"So that's it? Just like that?" she fidgeted with the salt shaker's top, afraid of the answer.

This is the type of conversation you might overhear on a train or in a restaurant. It makes little sense out of context, but to the participants it is rife with nuance and subtle sparring. You likely couldn't drop your readers into this conversation without some background, but with the proper build up you can craft a conversation between two characters who each have different agendas and create a subtext throughout the conversation. One more point about non-responsive dialogue: it is agenda driven; it's about characters expressing and pursuing what they want. So it's a great way for you the author to reveal and develop your characters.

There are numerous ways of presenting dialogue and a few conventions. The simplest way is to use quotes.

> *"Dinner will be late," he said. "I'm sorry, it took longer than I thought."*

> *"You always have some excuse, don't you?" she replied.*

Note that the quotation marks are outside the comma ending the sentence and the period goes after the tag line—the identification of who was speaking—but that a question ends with a question mark inside the quotes, and then the tag line.

Some writers prefer to use an *em dash* to separate speakers.

> *—Dinner will be late, he said. I'm sorry, it took longer than I thought.*

> *—You always have some excuse, don't you? she replied.*

Some writers use no tag lines or quotation marks at all.

> *Dinner will be late. I'm sorry it took longer than I thought.*

> *You always have some excuse, don't you?*

In any of these cases always give each speaker his own paragraph. Sometimes it's very hard to keep track of who is speaking in a dialogue. Separating the speakers by paragraph helps your reader stay in the scene.

Dialogue sets two characters in motion and brings the reader into an event, a scene. When you are writing your story, you'll know the moments that are the most important. These are the ones you want to create scenes for rather than simply using exposition, narrative. Remember we said that Heller showed us the profound and told us the mundane? This is the same situation. Tell me what I need to know about a situation and then show me what it means or how it affects the characters or the plot.

Let's look at a scene from Joseph Roth's novel *The Radetzky March*. The two characters are the District Captain, named Baron von Trotta, and the aged valet Jacques who is for the first time the Baron can remember, too sick to come to work. The Baron has come to visit Jacques in his cabin on the grounds of the manor after learning from the doctor that Jacques is dying.

> *The district captain sat on a bedside chair and said, "Well, the doctor's just told it's not so bad. Probably a cold in the head."*
>
> *"Yessir, Herr Baron," replied Jacques, making a feeble attempt to click his heels under the blanket. He sat up. "Please forgive me," he added. "I think it will be over by tomorrow."*
>
> *"Within a couple of days, I am sure of it!"*
>
> *"I'm waiting for the priest, Herr Baron."*
>
> *"Yes, yes," said Herr von Trotta, "he'll be coming. There's more than enough time."*
>
> *"He's already on his way," replied Jacques, as if with his own eyes he could see the priest approaching. "He's coming," he went on, and suddenly he seemed no longer aware that the district captain was sitting next to him. "When the late Herr Baron passed away, " he continued, "none of us knew anything. That morning, or maybe it was the previous day, he came into the courtyard and said 'Jacques, where are the boots?'. Yes, it was the day before. And the next*

morning he didn't need them anymore. The winter set in right away, it was a very cold winter. I think I'll make it to winter. Winter isn't that far away. I just need a little patience. It's July now, so July, June, May, April, August, November and by Christmas I think I'll be able to go out."

There is so much happening here, it's hard to know where to start. Roth sets up the scene in an earlier paragraph by telling the reader that von Trotta, the district captain, has never been to Jacques's cottage although Jacques has served the von Trotta family for 30 years. But he shows us the relationship when Jacques feebly attempts to click his heels in the presence of the baron. This is telling the mundane and showing the profound.

The dialogue here works the same way. Von Trotta knows that Jacques is dying but opens the conversation with hopeful words. Jacques works hard in the opening lines but begins to fade. Roth tells us this when he notes that Jacques no longer seemed to know the Baron is present. But Roth shows us that Jacques is fading through the dialogue (non-responsive dialogue at this point) when Jacques begins rambling about the death of the former Baron and about his own mortality. So it's not shocking when Jacques loses the sequence of the months, but it is still powerful.

The moment where Jacques feebly tries to click his heels in an expression of respect is a remarkable gesture. It shows so much about their relationship. But gestures can serve purposes in dialogue beyond demonstration. They can also be used to insert a beat, a quick pause, into a conversation. Beat is a musical term and writers use it purposefully as a way of adding the concept of rhythm to prose writing. In this case, what we call a beat is a description of some physical action or event placed between spoken lines of dialogue.

There are any number of ways to do this. You could add facial expressions— a furrowed or raised eyebrow not only demonstrates a character's frame of mind but also changes the rhythm of a conversation. Actions like pursed lips, tightening a jaw or narrowing a gaze can indicate a change in the temperature of the exchange. Classic, well-understood signals like eyes darkening and face reddening signal anger while a real smile signals happiness or joy and a Pan-Am smile signals something entirely different. Actors use facial expressions to signal emotion, watch the good ones and you'll figure out how to do it in your writing.

People also tend to talk with their hands or fidget with things in their hands when they talk. Your characters can point a finger, unscrew the saltshaker's top, drum their fingers or form them into a steeple. You might have a character throw up her hands in frustration just before or during a verbal explosion.

In the court martial scene in his classic *The Caine Mutiny*, Herman Wouk uses some of these techniques to both demonstrate the character's frame of mind and adjust the pace of the dialogue. Lieutenant Keefer is under examination in the trial of another officer, Lieutenant Maryk, who is charged with mutiny. The President of the Court, Captain Blakely, speaks first.

> *"Were you surprised, two weeks later, when he relieved the   captain?"*
>
> *"I was flabbergasted."*
>
> *"Were you pleased, Mr. Keefer?"*
>
> *Keefer squirmed in his chair, peered at the fierce face of Blakely, and said, "I've said that Maryk was my close friend..."*

This one action, squirming in his chair, might seem a little cliché, but it works well to show us that Keefer is uncomfortable. After all he has just been asked if he was pleased when his captain was relieved of command by the executive officer in combat—but it also inserts a bit of a pause into the dialogue. We can see the officer squirm a bit and then pause to peer at the face of the judge while we're waiting to hear his response. This creates just a bit more tension for the reader.

Here's one more example from Tobias Wolff. This is from his short story *Soldier's Joy,* there are three principal characters: Hooper, Porchoff, and Trac. Porchoff is thinking of killing himself while on guard duty, Hooper is the corporal of the guard. This is near the climax. Hooper and Porchoff are at an outdoor table.

> *"Let's call it a day," Hooper said. He stood and held out his hand. "Give me the rifle."*
>
> *"No," said Porchoff. He pulled the rifle closer. "Not to you."*
>
> *"There's no one here but me."*
>
> *"Go get Captain King."*
>
> *"Captain King is asleep."*
>
> *"Then wake him up."*
>
> *"No," Hooper said. "I'm not going to tell you again, Porchoff, give me your rifle." Hooper walked around toward him but stopped when Porchoff picked up the weapon and pointed at his chest. "Leave me alone," Porchoff said.*
>
> *"Relax," Hooper told him. "I'm not going to hurt you." He held out his hand again.*
>
> *Porchoff licked his lips. "No," he said. "Not you."*
>
> *Behind Hooper a voice called out, "Hey! Porkchop! Drop it!"*
>
> *Porchoff sat bolt upright. "Jesus," he said.*

"It's Trac," Hooper said. "Put the rifle down Porchoff —now!"

"Oh, Jesus," Porchoff said and stumbled to his feet with the rifle still in his hands." ...

The scene continues and, predictably, doesn't end well. But the point of reading it here is to show how Wolff uses gesture and movement. Hooper's motion initiates the climax of the story. Wolff has Hooper say, "Lets call it a day," and then stand and hold out his hand. He balances this movement and gesture with Porchoff's reaction to pull the rifle closer to himself. Imagine watching this play out. Hooper's hand reaches towards Porchoff and Porchoff pulls back into himself—a balanced reaction. The next movement and gesture is when Hooper moves around towards Porchoff. This is a bigger movement and gets an equally big, and balanced reaction, Porchoff points the rifle at Hooper's chest.

Then, Wolff goes in close and intensely personal. Hooper says, "Relax," and holds out his hand. Porchoff's reaction to this very small gesture is unbalanced, he licks his lips, he's withdrawing further into himself. This seems to throw the entire scene out of balance and things accelerate, the volume goes up— note the use of exclamation points. So when Trac begins yelling, Porchoff sits bolt upright and things go badly from that point on. Wolff uses movement and gesture amid dialogue to slow the scene down, to put a beat or two into the dialogue and to create balance and imbalance between the characters.

Just a couple more things on dialogue and then we can move on, and his next bit is one of the more valuable bits of craft to grasp, so stay with me. We're going to again categorize dialogue. We set out three types at the beginning: expository, responsive and non-responsive. So let's set three different categories: direct, indirect and free indirect.

Direct is simple quoted speech, it looks like this:

> *Williams laid his helmet on the fender and thought about what had just happened. "What the hell am I supposed to do now?" he asked of no one in particular.*

The narrator tells us something—sets the stage for us—and then we 'hear' Williams' words. They are presented in a direct quote, exactly as he spoke them. It is direct.

Indirect or reported speech looks like this:

> *Williams laid his helmet on the fender and thought about what had just happened. He wondered out loud what he was supposed to do next.*

Again, the narrator tells us something. But this time the narrator tells us what Williams said rather than quoting him. It is reported to us, thus indirect.

Free indirect dialogue looks like this:

> *Williams laid his helmet on the fender and thought about what had just happened. What the hell was he supposed to do now?*

Notice how this reads. There are no quotation marks, no tag lines (*he said, she asked*). It's not immediately clear if you're in Williams's head or if you're reading the narrator's commentary. But in fact, you are inside Williams' head. He could just as easily have pondered, *What the hell am I supposed to do now?* It is internal dialogue: Williams speaking to himself or thinking.

You can find some better examples of free indirect style than I've created here. Look at this from Kingsley Amis's novel *Lucky Jim.*

> *Dixon agreed rather than disagree with Beesley, but he didn't feel interested enough to*

say so. It was one of those days when he felt quite convinced of his impending expulsion from academic life. What would he do afterwards? Teach in a school? Oh dear no. Go to London and get a job in an office. What job? Whose office? Shut up.

Dixon is the Lucky Jim of the title and he's a bit anxious about losing his job. But the point is that throughout Lucky Jim, Amis seamlessly slips into a free indirect style to give us an idea of what Dixon is thinking and feeling; it allows Amis to show us the differences between what Dixon says and what he wants to say—the space in between the two is irony.

There is also this from Somerset Maugham's short story "Red":

Neilson watched him make his way across and when he had disappeared among the coconuts he looked still. Then he sank heavily in his chair. Was that the man who had prevented him from being happy? Was that the man whom Sally had loved all these years and for whom she had waited so desperately? It was grotesque. A sudden fury seized him so that he had an instinct to spring up and smash everything around him. He had been cheated. They had seen each other at last and had not known it. He began to laugh, mirthlessly, and his laughter grew till it became hysterical. The Gods had played him a cruel trick. And he was old now.

At last Sally came in to tell him dinner was ready. He sat down in front of her and tried to eat. He wondered what she would say if he told her now that the fat old man sitting in the chair was the lover whom she remembered still with the passionate abandonment of her youth. Years ago, when he hated her because she made him so unhappy, he would have been glad to tell her. He wanted to hurt her then as she hurt him, because his hatred was only love. But now he did not care. He shrugged his shoulders listlessly.

"What did that man want?" she asked presently.

He did not answer at once. She was old too, a fat old native woman. He wondered why he had ever loved her so madly. He had laid at her feet all the treasures of his soul, and she had cared nothing for them. Waste, what waste! And now, when he looked at her, he felt only contempt. His patience was at last exhausted.

Maugham mixes narration with free indirect speech and direct speech but it is more noticeable here than in Amis's paragraph above. In Maugham's first paragraph, the free indirect speech comes quickly—in the third and fourth sentences. Notice that the narrator is speaking to us and then we are inside the protagonist's head: *Was that the man who had prevented him from being happy? Was that the man whom Sally had loved for all those years and for whom she had waited so desperately?* Note that there are no quotation marks or tag lines like *He thought*, or *He wondered*. Then, in the very next sentence, we're back to narration: *It was grotesque.*

Maugham's middle paragraph is pure narration. Note the use of tag lines, *He wondered...* After the direct speech, the quoted line *"What did that man want?" she asked presently,* Maugham then goes right back to mixed speech with four sentences of narration followed by one short blast of free indirect speech, *Waste, what waste!* And then he finishes with narration.

In our earlier categorizations (expository, responsive and non-responsive), we were getting at the way the author uses dialogue to present his characters in action—remember speaking and thinking are actions—and how the author uses dialogue as a tool in managing time. When we discuss the latter categories (direct, indirect, free indirect), we're deciding how far into the head of the characters the author allows the reader to go, and how the author enables that access.

The free indirect style of discourse brings us fully into the character's mind in a way that appears seamless. If it is done correctly, the reader doesn't feel the shift from narrator to character: it combines elements of first- and third person. It is the most cohesive way of presenting your characters: it gives the reader the most access to the character; and the most inclusive: because the reader is party to the character's thoughts, the character's actions, and the things the narrator tells us, the reader is empowered, trusted, and more deeply engaged.

Finally, there's something about well-crafted dialogue that you should always notice: It sounds real. The bad expository dialogue at the front of this chapter didn't sound real. So how can you make sure your dialogue does sound real. Well here are a few tips:

—First, listen. How do people talk? They talk mostly in ways that seem to a passer by as non-responsive because they enjoy context that is unknown to others. You don't need to tell your best friend that you never thought *Seinfeld* was funny because your friend knows this about you. This is context. How do you get this? When you're out and about in town, take a minute once in a while to listen to people having a conversation. Really listen to how they speak to each other and try to imagine how well they know each other. This is a good head start on understanding how your characters will speak to each other.

—Then, understand that as a writer you can't reproduce exactly the flow of a conversation with all of its interjections (*um, er, you know, like, <grunt>*) and non-verbals. You have to find the happy medium between the way people really talk and the way it looks, sounds and feels best reproduced on the page.

—Next, when you think you have it right, read it aloud. That's the best way to know if a dialogue feels real or not is to verbalize it, read it out loud. How do the pauses, the beats, you've built in fit? Does one character have too much of the dialogue? Is it balanced in a way that is believable? For example, in a discussion between a drill sergeant and a recruit, the recruit might have very short responses of "Yes, Sergeant" and "No, Sergeant." But the NCO could have considerably more to say. This is unbalanced but in a believable way.

Finally, you should choose carefully when to use dialogue. You want to use dialogue to show the profound, of course, whether that's the relationship between two people strengthening or crumbling, or if it's to allow one of your characters to demonstrate some character trait or flaw. But you want to use it to advance your story, your plot. Which sets us up to move onto the next chapter, scene.

Exercises:

1. Take a break. Okay, not really. But go sit somewhere like a coffee shop or a bus depot or train station. Eavesdrop on a conversation. That is, listen to what people say. Write down what people are actually saying including all the starts and stops and ums and likes and whatevers. Write all of this out in dialogue form. Then decide what you can safely cut out while still leaving your reader with a clear idea of what's happening.

2. Write out a dialogue between two people, but only the words they would each say. Let it go on for about one page. Then go in and add the tag lines and stage directions. Notice how the additions make this into a much more interesting piece to read?

3. Write a piece of dialogue between two characters who have just met in the waiting room of a dentist. One is an extrovert and the other not. Have them chat about something that has just been shown on the TV. Write this is direct dialogue. Then re-write it in indirect form from the point of view of one of the characters - the one who is an introvert.

SCENE

We noted earlier that a short story was a piece of fiction of a certain length in which one significant event happens. You can think of scenes in this way, too. A scene is a moment in your story when something of consequence happens. Scenes are the vehicles you use to move your plot, your characters, your story forward in some significant way.

In dialogue, exposition is the stuff you put in the spaces between what your characters say. In the larger work exposition is the stuff between the scenes.

If you can imagine your story as a house, think of scenes as room in that house. Scenes have purpose, just like rooms do. You only have sufficient space in the house for a certain number of rooms and each has a specific purpose. So, too, you'll need to fit a certain number of scenes into your story and each of them should have value and meaning.

So I've just given you three different ways to think about scenes. But how do scenes work and how should you use them?

We'll try to answer that question with a look at the way three different writers handle the same or similar events. Let's start with a scene from Stendhal's *The Charterhouse of Parma*. The two characters are Fabrizio, a young Italian nobleman who has left home to fight in the Napoleonic wars, and a camp follower identified only as the Cantinière.

> *The Cantinière turned to the right and took a side road that ran through the fields; there was a foot of mud in it; the little cart seemed about to be stuck fast: Fabrizio pushed the wheel. His horse fell twice; presently the road, though with less water on it, was nothing more than a bridle path through the grass. Fabrizio had not gone five hundred yards when his nag stopped short: it was a corpse, lying across the path, which terrified horse and rider alike.*

> *Fabrizio's face, pale enough by nature, assumed a markedly green tinge; the Cantinière, after looking at the dead man, said, as though speaking to herself: "That's not one of our Division." Then, raising her eyes to our hero, she burst out laughing.*

> *"Aha, my boy! There's a tidbit for you!" Fabrizio sat frozen. What struck him most of all was the dirtiness of the feet of this corpse which had already been stripped of its shoes and left with nothing but an old pair of trousers all clotted with blood.*

> *"Come nearer," the Cantinière ordered him, "get off your horse, you'll have to get accustomed to them; look," she cried, "he's stopped one in the head."*

> *A bullet, entering on one side of the nose, had gone out at the opposite temple, and disfigured the corpse in a hideous fashion. It lay with one eye still open.*

"Get off your horse then, lad," said the Cantinière, "and give him a shake of the hand to see if he'll return it."

Without hesitation, although ready to yield up his soul with disgust, Fabrizio flung himself from his horse and took the hand of the corpse which he shook vigorously; then he stood still as though paralysed. He felt that he had not the strength to mount again. What horrified him more than anything was that open eye.

Look closely at a couple things. First, the way Stendhal sets the scene. He gives us place, description and action, then he describes Fabrizio's physical and emotional state, before he begins the dialogue. He allows us to situate ourselves in a place and to understand what the actors are doing before he starts the scene.

Next, think about the language describing Fabrizio's response to the dead man. His face is green, he is frozen, he is ready to yield up his soul in disgust. But he takes up the challenge—he shakes the dead man's hand.

Now let's look at a similar scene in Stephen Crane's *The Red Badge of Courage.*

At length he reached a place where the high, arching boughs made a chapel. He softly pushed the green doors aside and entered. Pine needles were a gentle brown carpet. There was a religious half light.

Near the threshold he stopped, horror-stricken at the sight of a thing.

He was being looked at by a dead man who was seated with his back against a column-like tree. The corpse was dressed in a uniform that had once been blue, but was now faded to a melancholy shade of green. The eyes, staring at the youth, had changed to the dull hue to be seen on the side of a dead fish. The mouth was open. Its red had changed to an appalling yellow. Over the gray skin of the face ran little ants. One was trundling some sort of bundle along the upper lip.

The youth gave a shriek as he confronted the thing. He was for moments turned to stone before it. He remained staring into the liquid-looking eyes. The dead man and the living man exchanged a long look. Then the youth cautiously put one hand behind him and brought it against a tree. Leaning upon this he retreated, step by step, with his face still toward the thing. He feared that if he turned his back the body might spring up and stealthily pursue him.

The branches, pushing against him, threatened to throw him over upon it. His unguided feet, too, caught aggravatingly in brambles; and with it all he received a subtle suggestion to touch the corpse. As he thought of his hand upon it he shuddered profoundly.

At last he burst the bonds which had fastened him to the spot and fled, unheeding the underbrush. He was pursued by the sight of black ants swarming greedily upon the gray face and venturing horribly near to the eyes.

After a time he paused, and, breathless and panting, listened. He imagined some strange voice would come from the dead throat and squawk after him in horrible menaces.

The trees about the portal of the chapel moved soothingly in a soft wind. A sad silence was upon the little guarding edifice.

Crane similarly sets the scene for us, although Crane moves us more quickly to the meat of the scene. Henry Fleming has fled his unit in the face of a concerted Confederate assault. He arrives at a nearby wood and encounters a dead and decomposing Union soldier. Then Crane gives us the description of the corpse and Henry's reaction to it: This time the soldier's face not the protagonist's is green but Henry, like Fabrizio is frozen in place by the sight. While he might not be ready to yield up his soul, he shrieks in surprise and shudders profoundly. Note, too, that both Stendhal and Crane focus on their protagonist's reaction to the dead man's eye(s).

The similarities aside, there is one enormous difference between these scenes: Crane's has no dialogue. Young Henry Fleming is alone while Fabrizio is accompanied by his *Cantinière*. Does this make a difference in the effectiveness of the scene? Can this actually be a scene without dialogue?

Well, my answers are no, it doesn't make any difference to me, and yes, it actually is a scene. But what does this tell us about scenes? Probably just what we described above—that a scene is a moment in the story when something of consequence happens. No more, no less. You can build scenes more easily with dialogue, I think. But Crane has demonstrated that it's not an absolute requirement.

These scenes also demonstrate something nearly universal about writing the military experience—at least about writing the combat experience—that confronting death is significant. In both of these cases, the living person confronts death away from the battlefield and the dead man is unknown to the living man. In both of these cases this confrontation take places early in the wartime experience of the soldier and early in the story. The moment has gravity or it wouldn't have been made a scene. The authors are steeling their protagonists to the sight of death.

Now let's look at how these authors signal us as readers that these are significant moments? Somehow, we as readers know or maybe feel that these moments have significance while we're reading our way into the scene. But how? Well, short sentences and phrases for one thing. Each of these authors uses short sentences and phrases—six or seven words average—to tell the stories here. This does a couple of things. Primarily, it slows you the reader down. Every time you come to a period your brain hesitates or even stops momentarily. You've been programmed to do this since you were first learning to read. A period is a stop sign, so you stop for just a tick. The net effect of this is to make your brain behave like your car does when you're driving in a residential neighborhood: You never really have time to get up any speed. Your brain takes each sentence or phrase in the paragraph like your car takes each block in the neighborhood.

This opens us up to a discussion of how time moves in scenes and more broadly in any story. First, we need to consider how time passes within a story. For example, a story in a novel could take place over the period of a dozen years. But that time is compressed, otherwise it would take you a dozen years to read the story. Time is compressed through the use of exposition or summary. So let's call the different types of time in a story scene/discourse time and exposition/summary time.

In exposition or summary, the passage of time can be compressed or extended. It can also be unclear or irrelevant. It is not equal to real time.

In discourse, we watch the scene as it plays out in front of us. We watch and feel the time passing as the characters speak, move, point, eat, drive or do whatever the author has them doing. We see it happen with our own eyes. Discourse time is equal to real time.

Stendhal's opening paragraph doesn't really have a time marker in it. The *Cantinière* turns down a muddy road and there is a cart stuck in the mud. We later learn the two travel only about 500 yards, not very far really. But we never get a clear idea how long this takes. This is summary time. But when they begin to speak, we change to discourse time. From that point on, the story time equals real time.

The physical presence, or stage direction, here is important, too. In both of these scenes the living character winds up too close to a dead body and revulsion forces a hasty withdrawal. That proximity forces us, the readers, into that space, too. It's pretty uncomfortable. But more importantly, because these are consequential moments, the authors slow things down for us.

Finally, on these two scenes, there are some things I'd like to see that aren't here. For one, smell. Dead bodies smell. Stendahl, who wrote *Charterhouse* after his combat experience would no doubt have known this. But he inexplicably leaves out the repellent stench of death. Crane, who had no combat experience before writing *Badge* might not have known this. I think they both do well at creeping the reader out with the senses—both have the living either touch or shudder at the idea of touching the dead. But I think smell is so powerful a sensation, especially the smell of the dead, and I think they goof by omitting it.

OK, moving on. Let's look at two other scenes. First up is one of the best known scenes in Tolstoy's *War and Peace*: the Lofty Sky scene.

> *On the Pratzen Heights, where he had fallen with the flagstaff in his hand, lay Prince Andrew Bolkonski bleeding profusely and unconsciously uttering a gentle, piteous, and childlike moan.*
>
> *Toward evening he ceased moaning and became quite still. He did not know how long his unconsciousness lasted. Suddenly he again felt that he was alive and suffering from a burning, lacerating pain in his head.*
>
> *"Where is it, that lofty sky that I did not know till now, but saw today?" was his first thought. "And I did not know this suffering*

either," he thought. "Yes, I did not know anything, anything at all till now. But where am I?"

He listened and heard the sound of approaching horses, and voices speaking French. He opened his eyes. Above him again was the same lofty sky with clouds that had risen and were floating still higher, and between them gleamed blue infinity. He did not turn his head and did not see those who, judging by the sound of hoofs and voices, had ridden up and stopped near him.

It was Napoleon accompanied by two aides-de-camp. Bonaparte riding over the battlefield had given final orders to strengthen the batteries firing at the Augesd Dam and was looking at the killed and wounded left on the field.

"Fine men!" remarked Napoleon, looking at a dead Russian grenadier, who, with his face buried in the ground and a blackened nape, lay on his stomach with an already stiffened arm flung wide.

"The ammunition for the guns in position is exhausted, Your Majesty," said an adjutant who had come from the batteries that were firing at Augesd.

"Have some brought from the reserve," said Napoleon, and having gone on a few steps he stopped before Prince Andrew, who lay on his back with the flagstaff that had been dropped beside him. (The flag had already been taken by the French as a trophy.)

"That's a fine death!" said Napoleon as he gazed at Bolkonski.

Prince Andrew understood that this was said of him and that it was Napoleon who said it. He heard the speaker addressed as Sire. But he heard the words as he might have heard the buzzing of a fly. Not only did they not interest him, but he took no notice of them and at once forgot them. His head was burning, he felt himself bleeding to death, and he saw above him the remote, lofty, and everlasting sky. He knew it was Napoleon—his hero—but at that moment Napoleon seemed to him such a small, insignificant creature compared with what was passing now between himself and that lofty infinite sky with the clouds flying over it. At that moment it meant nothing to him who might be standing over him, or what was said of him; he was only glad that people were standing near him and only wished that they would help him and bring him back to life, which seemed to him so beautiful now that he had today learned to understand it so differently. He collected all his strength, to stir and utter a sound. He feebly moved his leg and uttered a weak, sickly groan which aroused his own pity.

"Ah! He is alive," said Napoleon. "Lift this young man up and carry him to the dressing station."

Having said this, Napoleon rode on to meet Marshal Lannes, who, hat in hand, rode up smiling to the Emperor to congratulate him on the victory.

Prince Andrew remembered nothing more: He lost consciousness from the terrible pain of being lifted onto the stretcher, the jolting while being moved, and the probing of his wound at the dressing station.

Okay, now let's look at another scene from *The Charterhouse of Parma.*

Fabrizio counted four gold-laced hats. A quarter of an hour later, from a few words said by one hussar to the next, Fabrizio gathered that one of these generals was the famous Marshal Ney. His happiness knew no bounds; only he had no way of telling which of the four generals was Marshal Ney; he would have given everything in the world to know, but he remembered that he had been told not to speak. ...

He was thinking more of Marshal Ney and of glory than of his horse, which, being highly excited, jumped into the canal, ...

On reaching the farther bank, Fabrizio had found the generals there by themselves; the noise of the guns seemed to him to have doubled...

Fabrizio discovered that he was twenty paces on the generals' right front, and precisely in the direction in which they were gazing through their glasses. As he came back to take his place behind the other hussars, who had halted a few paces in rear of them, he noticed the biggest of these generals, who was speaking to his neighbour, a general also, in a tone of authority and almost of reprimand; he was swearing. Fabrizio could not contain his curiosity; and, in spite of the warning not to speak, given him by his friend the jailer's wife, he composed a short sentence in good French, quite correct, and said to his neighbour:

"Who is that general who is chewing up the one next to him?"

"Gad, it's the Marshal!"

"What Marshal?"

"Marshal Ney, you fool! I say, where have you been serving?"

Fabrizio, although highly susceptible, had no thought of resenting this insult; he was studying, lost in childish admiration, the famous Prince of Moscow, the 'Bravest of the Brave.'

...

He heard a sharp cry close to him; two hussars fell struck by shot; and, when he looked back at them, they were already twenty paces behind the escort. What seemed to him horrible was a horse streaming with blood that was struggling on the ploughed land, its hooves caught in its own entrails; it was trying to follow the others: its blood ran down into the mire.

"Ah! So I am under fire at last!" he said to himself. "I have seen shots fired!" he repeated with a sense of satisfaction. "Now I am a real soldier." At that moment, the escort began to go hell for leather, and our hero realised that it was shot from the guns that was making the earth fly up all round him. He looked vainly in the direction from which the balls were coming, he saw the white smoke of the battery at an enormous distance, and, in the thick of the

steady and continuous rumble produced by the artillery fire, he seemed to hear shots discharged much closer at hand: he could not understand in the least what was happening.

In both of these scenes, the protagonist is confronted with a great leader, someone he has admired. But that's really not the important part of the scene for us. The appearance of Napoleon and Ney provides a vehicle for these authors to demonstrate some aspect of character. Tolstoy shows us a soldier after a decisive battle during which he was wounded and in which his side was defeated. The Prince, gravely wounded and near death, begins to understand life in a way he didn't previously. Stendhal shows us a boy, keen for glory and wide-eyed at the sight of Marshal Ney. Both of these moments are of great consequence to the protagonist and thus to us the reader.

Scenes exist to demonstrate some necessary element of plot or character— something of consequence. If you're not familiar with the stories we're discussing here it will be difficult to answer questions like, "What's the author trying to do here?" So we can simply ask, "Where's the tension?"

Fabrizio has created his tension: he wants to be under fire, to become a soldier, and he wants to be in the presence of greatness, to be with Marshal Ney. So he foolishly takes chances, riding to the sound of the guns. He knows nothing of the flow of battle, so he puts himself between the cannons and the generals. His foolishness and ignorance creates tension: we wonder what mischief he can create.

For Prince Bolkonski, this is a life or death situation and he decides he wants to live. He is near death, contemplating his newly found understanding of the value and beauty of life, and hoping to live he summons the strength to let out a piteous sound. We wonder if the French will recognize that he is alive and what they might do to the enemy Prince.

Interestingly, both characters lose themselves to reverie in these scenes. The authors take us deep inside their thought processes. Remember that thinking is action.

Both scenes, as well as the earlier scenes with Henry Fleming's and Fabrizio's encounters with death, are moments of consequence for the protagonists. They are passages from one state of being to another, opportunities for the author to not only advance the story but to demonstrate significant elements of character through action. That, in a nutshell, is what scenes are all about.

Exercises:

1. Think of a day in your life, one of some consequence, as a collection of scenes. Write one quick scene from that day that includes some dialogue. Try to keep it to about a page but make it a complete scene with a beginning, middle, and end.

2. Write another scene from that day with no dialogue.

REVISION

This is the part of the book some people might assume they don't need to read and will skip through or over. After all, if you can write a first draft, what's so hard about revising it to become a final? It's the same process right?

Well, not so much. Revision is as much a process as any other part of writing. It is literally a re-visioning, a re-seeing of the work. You'll be looking at it with a different eye. It's not copy editing, just looking at grammar and punctuation. It is revision, revising the entire work to make it better. It requires certain skills and a degree of courage. This is the point where you have to go bravely back into the story and make hard decisions about plot and character, point of view and scene. Are there too many characters? Is the point of view inconsistent? Does the plot work?

Earlier, we said that it's not necessary to know precisely where your story will end up while you're writing the early parts. Sometimes, quite often actually, a story unfolds to the writer as it is being written. Characters become more interesting, plotlines converge, stuff happens. Once you've reached the final period, take a break, save the document and get away from it for a while.

Then, when you're ready to start revision—maybe this is a few hours later for a short work but for something major you should take at least a few days—do a few things right up front that will make your work easier. Save an extra copy of the document as the baseline from which you'll be working. It's always interesting to have an early draft around to look at, and things are so much easier with word processing than they were for writers who came before us. There is a story about our friend Isaac Babel presenting a sheaf of papers to a friend to read. The friend asks if the stack is a novel and Babel says no, it's 20 revisions of the same story.

Now, read through your story. Read closely. Look at the plot, the major scenes, the conflict and the characters. Outline the plot briefly to identify the major events and scenes. Use this outline to help you determine if the story really does what you intend it to do. Does the storyline make sense? Are there too many scenes or too many characters and plotlines?

If so, revise. You might re-write the scenes by compressing or expanding. Give the characters room to move through the story, to do things that add life to the action or the scene. Unchain them and yourself. At this point, don't sweat details like punctuation. This is work at the macro level. You're fixing the foundation of the story, not putting on the finishing touches. That will come later.

Now I said you could re-write the scenes by compressing or expanding. This gets to a fundamental element of how you write: Do you create by addition or subtraction? Think about a sculptor. Some sculptors create their art by chipping away at a block of marble until a statue emerges. This is subtraction. Some sculptors build something out of pieces. This is addition. In some ways revision is similar to sculpting. Some writer's drafts are dense and filled with detail, character motivation, discourse, metaphor and so on. These writers might start with a draft of 500 pages. The revision process for them is subtraction. They work to take out the extraneous, the disruptive, the distracting.

The motto here might be that perfection isn't when there is nothing left to say; it's when there is nothing left to cut.

Other writers sketch out just the bare bones of a story in first draft. Their characters might lack back-story; their scenes might have only the basic elements of dialogue without stage direction or body language. Perhaps there aren't a sufficient number of scenes to advance the narrative to the climax or the scenes in place don't fully develop tension or display motivation. This type of writer needs to revise through addition, expanding the story, plot, dialogue, whatever absences are weakening the whole.

There are numerous models for thinking about revision. In one, you might think of writing as occurring in three stages: madman, architect, editor. Your first draft is the madman stage: just get the ideas out onto the page. Write and write, don't look back.

The second stage, architect, is macro-revision. This is where you're insuring that the story has a strong foundation: that the scenes all fit and are well constructed. That is the first revision. It's important to say here that first revision doesn't mean one quick shot through and you're done. No, this can go on in multiple rounds and versions until you're satisfied, or until your agent, editor or publisher is satisfied that you've gotten the story right.

Finally, you'll reach the editor stage where you can really tighten down all the bolts. This is where you have a chance to use everything we've learned in this course. You can create a checklist if you want of things to go through, but a glance back through this book will also serve as a reminder.

Another model is to work in four distinct stages. The first stage is simply getting the story onto the page. Here you discover whose story it is from start to finish.

In the second stage you expand on what you have and look for opportunities to develop the story, to dig into characters and evaluate the structure and the plot—the order in which you've set the main elements. Here's where you give the story a once over looking for all the elements of craft.

The third stage is the longest and most detailed look. Here you're going to really dig into details within the story: specific moments, problem areas, missing points or events. You'll clarify things that are muddy, track the main and other important characters from end to end. You'll also track all the minor characters to make sure there aren't any loose ends. Here is where you have to insure that you have nailed down the theme.

Finally, in the fourth stage, you've got to go through and polish up the prose. Make sure you read the entire piece aloud and fix the rough spots you come across. Then proofread for spelling and grammar.

Here's a list of things you can ask yourself as you're moving through the different stages of revision.

—What's your theme? What is your story about? Is that clear to you? If it's not clear to you it's unlikely it will be clear to the reader.

—What's the structure of the story? Are the sections laid out in a way that leads the reader towards a climax and a denouement? Is it balanced? In other words do you spend the correct amount of time on the important stuff or did you go off on tangents and delay some major event so you could expound on something trivial?

—What is the plot? How does the story unfold? Does it unfold in a logical way with a beginning, a middle and an end? It doesn't have to be linear—this happened, then this and finally that. But it does have to be logical. This gets to things like timing and placement of scenes and action. You can't have someone leap out of an airplane before they board for example.

—Are the characters real or at least realistic? Do they act in ways that seem reasonable, even if they are being irrational? Are your principal characters round? If not, make them so. Are your minor characters stereotypes? If so, fix them. Do your characters have desires?

—What is the point of view? Is it consistent? Even if you change your point of view during the story, it needs to remain consistent at each moment. Are you using the correct point of view? Could you better tell the story from a different point of view?

—How is the setting? Does it support what you're doing? Have you sufficiently defined it? Is it a major part of your story, and if so, is its role clear?

—Does your story start at the right place? Does the opening grab your readers' attention and make them want to know what happens to your characters? Does you ending tie up all the loose ends satisfactorily?

—Is the voice consistent?

—Is the dialogue right? Read through your characters' words most carefully. Read them out loud. Do they sound believable? Is there enough or too much talk? This part really needs to pass the Goldilocks test.

—Are your metaphors fresh or stale?

—Are you telling and showing?

—Do your descriptions use all five senses—taste, smell, touch, hearing and sight?

—Have you said things in the best way? Do you use more Germanic words than Latinate? Have you used more active voice than passive?

—Is the punctuation and grammar correct? I said early on in this book that it was not a handbook on grammar or punctuation and suggested that you get one and make it your friend. Here's the point where you need it. Copy-edit yourself to death. Fix the comma splices and the semi-colon gaffes. Make sure your tenses are consistent.

So just a few last things. I mentioned reading your dialogue out loud. This is a technique that can be helpful for both summary and scene. Read everything you've written out loud. Remember, you've written and re-written this in your head and on your laptop so many times by now that you might not see problems. Reading out loud is the closest you'll get to having the experience of reading for the first time. So read out loud and when you come to a point where you're stumbling over words, make note of it. You might need to clean up that passage. If you're getting bored or losing your focus, imagine how your reader will feel. Fix it. Having someone else to this either with your or for you can also be helpful.

And finally, we talked earlier about revision requiring courage. Sometimes in the revision process you will be faced with the simple fact that one of your scenes or major events or even a favorite character is clogging up the story. In this case you have to do the honorable thing and kill off the character or excise the offending scene. It's hard to do. You've just spent hours or days or weeks crafting this character or scene into something beautiful, but if it doesn't work it doesn't work. Be brave and be bold. Cut. Revise.

Exercises:

1. Use these techniques to revise a piece you've written.

2. Do it again.

3. Don't stop revising until you're really convinced it is as good as it possibly can be.

WRITING ABOUT TRAUMA

Writing is, possibly more than anything else, an exercise of the imagination. Our mind allows us to create with language things that did not previously exist. I'm sure that neurologists and philosophers and artists would all have differing views on how this process works. But I think that it is the cumulative influence of our experiences that allow us to shape language into words, sentences paragraphs, dialogue, scenes and stories.

Yet some of the things we've seen and done never really become part of our day-to-day lives. Memories of some traumatic experiences, especially experiences from a war, may never become fully integrated with other memories. Those memories, those stories, stand apart from other experiences in our lives because they might involve actions antithetical to what we understand as accepted human interaction. The violence and destruction that occur in war: The killing and wounding, the inhumanity and hatred, can quite often be outside of our ability to understand. We see but we sometimes cannot process fully what we see because it is incomprehensible. And what we cannot comprehend, we cannot express.

But those memories do exist. They are always a part of us. We cannot change what has happened nor erase what we have seen and done.

Those of us who were participants face two distinct challenges: to manage our memories and to bear witness to others.

In the front pages of this book, I placed a quote by Vera Brittain that speaks to the need to repair the damages to the psyche of war experiences.

> *Only, I felt, by some such attempt to write history in terms of personal life could I rescue something that might be of value, some element of truth and hope and usefulness, from the smashing up of my own youth by the war.*

Brittain saw her memoir as a way to make sense of her experiences. She calls the work a rescue. Brittain was a nurse in the war and, I'm projecting here, I suspect she saw the writing she did as a type of therapy.

Undoubtedly, gaining better control over specific memories can be therapeutic. To be clear, I'm not a therapist. I am not a psychologist or a psychiatrist or a social worker. I have pretty much zero medical training in fact. I can only speak from my experience.

I was treated in Afghanistan for Post-Traumatic Stress Disorder. I was treated for what my psychiatrist called an Adjustment Disorder in the years that followed. I left the service and went to school to become a writer.

In my classes I tried to capture the stories of what I saw and experienced in places like Afghanistan, Iraq, Rwanda, Kosovo and Darfur. Honestly, sometimes it sucked to drag all of that stuff out again, to examine it and re-live the experiences. But every time I did, I gained a little more control over the memories. I began to feel like I could control each particular memory a bit more. Gradually, I began to feel like I was getting more control over my life.

I assumed there was some medical and scientific reason for this that I wouldn't understand because I'm neither a doctor nor a scientist. But I looked into it anyway and dug though some of the literature. Doctor James Pennebaker is a leader in this type of research. I started with his work and branched out as needed. The literature begins with a discussion of the process of therapeutic writing. Here are a few summarized points that I've shaped a bit to include my personal experience:

> —*Sit down to write for 15 to 30 minutes a day.*

> —*What you write about is important. If you're trying to get control of bad memories, writing about all the happy stuff isn't likely to help. You have to write about the bad stuff.*

> —*Explore several aspects of the event you're writing about: the event itself, how it changed you, your relationship with others (parent, friends, spouse/partner), your outlook on life, your job, how you view yourself, your past present and future. In other words, not just what happened but what happened afterwards.*

> —*Don't worry about spelling or grammar or structure. What's important is that you write for the full period of time you've allotted.*

> —*It's not important whether you show this to anyone or not. The value comes in the writing. You're writing for yourself, so be honest with yourself.*

But how does it help? Well, the literature is pretty technical on the "how" part. There are words and phrases in there like "blastogenesis procedure with mitogen phytohemogglutinin" (I am totally <u>not</u> making that up.). So I'll give you my ideas.

—*Through writing, you are creating something tangible. You can look at it. You can print it out and hold it in your hands. It is no longer something festering in the recesses of your memory.*

—*This airing often brings clarity. You force yourself to remember the event(s) and to sort through what really happened.*

—*By writing about something you can allow yourself to cede ownership of it. I think this is important because sometimes we tend to blame ourselves for things that were out of our control. It's a natural thing to do. We're programmed to do this. We look at some bad thing and something deep inside us says, "That's my fault. I should have done X, Y, or Z to stop it." Writing about an incident like this gives you a chance to absolve yourself of these feelings.*

—*Medically, according to Dr. Pennebaker, letting this stuff out reduces long-term stressors.*

—*Writing helps you put into words the indescribable. You force yourself to use metaphor to make sense of the inconceivable. This action is humanizing because the ability is uniquely human.*

—*By writing about significant emotional events and trauma you are building a framework around the memory and placing it under your control—rather than vice versa.*

Some of the "how" stuff I've listed above actually gets to the question of "why" as well. One of the questions I struggled with when I was first beginning to write my stories was why. I felt like I had all those bad memories stuffed into little boxes and hidden away under the bed pretty neatly. So why in the world would I want to open the boxes and play with those memories? Because they are going to come out sooner or later and it's better to bring them out on your own under conditions you can control than to have them start oozing out when you're not ready.

In my research I also had conversations with Dr. Robert Sapolsky at Stanford University and with Dr. Jonathan Shay from the VA hospital at Boston (both of these men have received MacArthur Fellowship grants—known as the Genius Grants) in trying to understand how memory works. Here's what I learned.

When you're involved in a traumatic event like a firefight (or a car crash or a violent physical assault) your brain goes into fight or flight mode. The big brain functions that make us human get pushed aside and a small part of your brain called the amygdula takes over. This happens to all mammals, by the way. This kind of event is life-threatening, so your brain views it as evolutionary—if you don't learn from it the species might not survive—so it is burned into the amygdula.

When we remember events, any events, the brain tries to reconstruct the exact processes involved during the original event. It access the visual cortex and the auditory cortex, and tries to have the same series of synapses fire. This is why some memories seem so realistic, as if you are re-living the moment.

This process is great for happy memories—like smelling a cinnamon bun or remembering playing catch with your dad. But for traumatic memories, not so much. Since your brain tries to recreate the exact same processes, it wants to tell your body to re-enact the flight or flight sensation: the brain tells the body to release chemicals like cortisol and adrenaline in order to function at the level needed to survive. In other words, you begin to re-live the moment—you have a flashback.

Writing, or any other of the creative arts, helps you control the memory because it forces you to re-engage the big part of your brain, the parts that deal with higher level functions, instead of leaving the re-construction to the lower functioning parts of the brain. My thinking is that this creates a filter to help control the memory. Like a glove allows you to pick up something hot, writing allows you to process a traumatic memory in a manageable way.

So that's the controlling the memories part of writing about trauma. What about the bearing witness part? The first quote in this book, by Justice Oliver Wendell Holmes, speaks to the idea of this duty to bear witness.

> *The generation that carried on the war has been set apart by its experience. Through our great good fortune, in our youth our hearts were touched with fire. It was given to us to learn that life is a profound and passionate thing. While we are permitted to scorn nothing but indifference, we have seen with our own eyes, and it is for us to bear the report to those who come after us.*

Holmes fought in the Civil War and this line is from a speech he gave at a Veterans Day event in 1884. Personally, I agree with Holmes. I think we have a duty to bear witness. As Holmes says, "it is for us to bear the report to those who come after us."

But not everyone feels this way. Lots of people will want to simply put the stories aside and leave them in the past. It is absolutely possible to close this stuff up inside yourself and hide it away. But if you've come this far in the program I have to believe that you intend to write your story, or at least a story.

By doing so, you are bearing witness. Putting what you write out in the public is further bearing witness and if you do so, you will join a long line of writers who have written about personal and societal trauma.

This is difficult work. As we noted just above, it challenges you to confront painful and disturbing memories. It is sometimes traumatic in itself to open these memories up and re-live them. But it is important to do so. Telling the stories, particularly from the perspective of someone who has lived the life, can help us give meaning to our actions and to those of our comrades-in-arms. It also gives participants a chance to explain to non-participants our experiences. Consider these few lines from Siegfried Sassoon's poem "Remorse":

> *Remembering how he saw those Germans run,*
> *Screaming for mercy among the stumps of trees:*
> *Green-faced, they dodged and darted: there was one*
> *Livid with terror, clutching at his knees...*
> *Our chaps were sticking 'em like pigs... "O hell!"*
> *He thought--"there's things in war one dare not tell*
> *Poor father sitting safe at home, who reads*
> *Of dying heroes and their deathless deeds."*

Sassoon is clearly addressing the divide between the soldier in the field and those sitting safely at home. But he is also getting at something more. Given the title of the poem, it seems to me that part of Sassoon's point is that warriors sometimes conduct themselves in ways that will cause them remorse partially because there are *"things in war one dare not tell poor father sitting safe at home."* But in fact these are the things that poor father sitting safe at home most needs to know. These are the things that non-combatants most need to understand. These things, and the horrific memories, remorse and regret that follow them are part of the human cost of war.

We write about these things to make sense of them. We have to write about them because they are too complex to understand simply inside our minds. How do you describe something like overcoming fear (or not) in close combat or under an artillery barrage? How can we even understand something as complex as the relationships that develop among a bomber crew in combat over Europe in 1944, or a platoon of Marines in Vietnam in 1971, or a cavalry troop in Iraq in 2005? No matter how we try to understand in inside, we all must know that these are things too complex to grasp all at once.

So we write. Line by line we create a narrative that puts into words—and perspective—the incomprehensible. A shorter work might help us understand one specific event or moment. A long, book-length narrative allows us to spread the issues or moments out, and helps us understand each of them individually. It will also allow us to keep them in context and in the process come to grasp a greater truth.

If you look back to the first chapter of the book, when I was explaining why we write, I wrote what can stand as the summary for this section: Some of us write because we need to figure things out and writing is one way of doing that. Putting the words down on paper helps us think through an event or a story and come to a better understanding of it. Sometimes we do this simply because we need to get the story out, to tell it and be done with it. Writing turns the ideas into something concrete, something physical that we can then push away from ourselves. It can give us distance. Sometimes we write to express things that can't be said out loud. We may have some sense or experience that can't be expressed directly. Writing allows us to create metaphors, one thing that substitutes for or represents another, and gives us the chance to express something unexplainable.

YOUR NEW LIFE AS A WRITER

Okay, that's it. We're through. You made it through the program. You're a graduate. Thanks for coming, I hope you got as much out of it as I did. Congratulations and good luck! See you around.

"But wait. What now?" you ask. Ah, now it's time to begin your new life as a writer. Yes, it's actually possible: you can have a new life as a writer.

First thing first: You should now stop saying, "I want to be a writer." Either you are or you're not. So make up your mind. If you are a writer, be sure about it and be clear. You are now authorized to say, "I am a writer." It doesn't matter if you ever have been or ever will be published. You are a writer because you write. If you're interested in publishing, you can do it and we will try to help you. If you're not interested in publishing, that doesn't change the fact that if you're writing, you're a writer.

But what does that mean, a new life as a writer? Well, it means you might end up changing your lifestyle a bit. If you're just starting out as a writer, it's likely you have other things going on in your life. Things like a job and a family. It is really likely that you're going to need to keep the day job for a while, or even forever. So if you're going to write, you're going to have to find time in your already busy life to do so.

This requires a bit of introspection. You need to look at your current lifestyle and ask when you can cut out a few minutes every day to write. This isn't easy. You have to find time away from your family and friends—the people who you count on for support and who count on you - to do your work. But you need to do it.

A few minutes a day might be enough. I know an author who wrote his first novel on the 25-minute train ride into his office and the same ride home in the evening. Yes, it took a while but he wrote it, sold it and moved on to write seven other books. Other writers put aside a few minutes first thing in the morning before the rest of the house is awake to sit and write while the house is quiet.

You need to find that time of day when you are going to be able to write. If you're demonstrably not a morning person, it might not be in the morning. Any time during the day when you can sit alone and get your work done is your time. Maybe it's at work during your lunch hour, or late at night or just before dinner. But you need some time and it should probably be the same time or as close to the same time each day.

You'll also need a place. This is sometimes the harder of the two needs. You need a place where you're not distracted, where you can focus on your work. I'm pretty lucky. I have a converted attic in my house that I use as a workspace. I have a desk, a pretty comfortable chair and a stack of books. I keep my laptop up there and I go up first thing every morning and write for half an hour. Maybe you can find a similar place in your house.

Or maybe it's not in your house at all. If you're part of the coffee shop culture, you know that there is an entire element of our society that seems to spend its day sitting in a coffee shop with a laptop open. I'm sure some of these folks are working on a novel or a memoir or an essay. If you can work in that environment, by all means do so. At this point it's all about you: Where can you work and when?

Maybe it's your public library. Make sure to ask about their policy on using computers, some libraries have specific areas where you can and can't click, click, click away on your laptop.

Some writers are lucky enough to keep a separate space for their work. I've heard of people keeping an apartment across town, a writing shed away from the main house, and using a friend's place to work. John Cheever, who we met in Chapter 1, got up and dressed in a suit each day, packed up a briefcase and went "to work." It apparently made him more cognizant of the fact that this was his job.

Regardless, you need a place and a time to write. Chances are that you've already identified both of these since you've made it this far into the program. So get to work!

Yes, I keep using that word, *work*. It is work and you ought to view it as work. This is something you do every day at the same time in the same place. It's very much like a job. You have to go to it every day, no excuses. It really doesn't matter what you write at first, it matters that you write. Go at it for 15 minutes or half an hour, then get up and go about your day. Come back the next day and do the same thing. Then, come back the next day and do the same thing. And then, come back the next day and do the same thing. You're trying to set a pattern in your life. You're trying to train your imagination to turn on at the same time every day. And soon it will. If this works for you, great. If not, try this.

Get a small notebook or a stack of index cards. Carry this (and a pen or pencil) with you where ever you go. When you think of something that adds to your story, take out the notebook or an index card and write it down. Keep this up until you're ready to start putting this together into a cohesive work. Of course, you could also do this on a handheld smart phone or a tablet or your laptop, but sometimes it's actually easier to always have a notebook or a card in your pocket. Think of this as simply exploiting every opportunity rather than locking yourself into habit. Some people simply work better spontaneously, without a regimen. If you're one of those people, maybe this is your method. And if neither of these systems work for you, keep at it. You'll find your own path somehow.

Beyond these lifestyle adjustments there are a few things you can do to improve your writing.

—Observe. At some point every day, take a minute to disengage with the rest of the world, sit back and watch, listen, smell and touch. Take note of the world around you in some higher degree of detail. Ask yourself, what does that resemble? What does this remind me of? What's that person doing and why? Then describe them in different ways. Work on making fresh metaphors.

—Read. Good writing is inspiring. Find authors you like and read their works. Then find out who they read and read that. Follow trails. Read things you don't think you'll like and if you really don't like it ask yourself why. What is it specifically that you don't like? Strive to be precise, be as articulate as you possibly can. Become articulate about your craft by becoming articulate about the craft of others. Deconstruct stories, novels, movies, television shows, every type of story to determine what makes it work well and where it can be improved.

—Share. This takes courage. Find a friend with whom you can share what you write. Make sure it's someone whose opinion you respect and who will be honest with you. Sometimes the best way to do this is to form or join a writers' group that workshops each others' work.

—Listen. When someone offers you criticism, take it. Listen to it and learn from it. If one of your writer friends says she thinks you use too many adjectives and your sentences are too long, say thanks and go back to your work to see if she's right. If five of your writer friends say you use too many adjectives and your sentences are too long, you might use too many adjectives and your sentences really might be too long.

—Write. This might be the most important advice you'll ever get: Just start writing and keep writing. You are a writer only if you actually do write. Don't wait until you have the time or you have the perfect idea or you've finished all your research. Start writing. You'll figure out what your research needs are pretty quickly and you will have started writing your story.

On getting your work out there.

Once your story is done—you've drafted and revised, read it out loud and fixed all the problems you've found—perhaps you'll want to put the story out for public consumption. Maybe this is why you want to be a writer in the first place, because you have some insight into the world and into the human condition that you want to share. Or maybe you just think your story needs to be told to a wider audience. Or maybe you want to try to make a living at this writing thing. For whatever reason, if you're ready to put your work into the public eye, here are some things to keep in mind.

First, remember that the world isn't seeking another writer. Editors and publishers are overwhelmed with writers trying to fill the shelves of the bookstore with their novels and memoirs, short story collections, and poetry chapbooks. So if you want to get published, your work will have to do two things: Meet the conventions to get in the door, and be different enough to stand out from the others.

Meeting the conventions means simply finding out in what format the specific magazine, publishing house, website or journal expects their submissions to arrive. Almost every venue accepts electronic submissions these days. Some only accept electronic submissions. Read the submission guidelines on the website or in the magazine and follow them precisely for formatting and timing. There is probably no faster way to avoid getting a good, fair evaluation of your work than to present a sloppy submission. It allows the editor to believe that you aren't familiar with the magazine and, quite honestly, don't really care. You're likely to wind up rejected out of hand. Most journals have reading periods when they accept submissions. If you miss the window, your work won't even be opened.

Standing out from the crowd is much more ethereal. If there is one great tip to making your work stand out I wish someone would give it to me. I queried a few editors, publishers and agents and found out that there is no single thing they look for. There are a few important items that were on everyone's lists. Perhaps most often, people said they wanted new, fresh ideas and particularly fresh language— metaphors and descriptions particularly. Important tip here: In fact, what sets us apart is simply what sets us apart. Maturing as a writer means becoming more one's self. Being true to one's own sense of story, of characters, of the way things feel, of what has meaning, is going to give you that fresh, honest, real sense. Look inward rather than outward for the new.

I would add that if your work is riddled with typographical, punctuation and grammatical errors readers become weary very quickly. Read, re-read and read aloud. Then, make sure you're sending your piece to the right place. Don't bother sending a piece about monster truck racing to Vogue unless you've got the killer angle that every Vogue reader will immediately grasp. If you find that angle, let me know.

Once you submit, be prepared to wait for a response. This could take a while, so be patient. Once your response comes, be prepared for rejection. Everyone gets rejected some. J.D. Salinger was rejected out of hand by the New Yorker for years. Once he finally got in, he stayed in. But there were a lot of rejection slips on the way. Many editors have a standardized response that goes something like this: *Thank you for your interest in XYZ magazine. We read your submission carefully but found that it doesn't fit with our current needs.* Maybe this is a blow-off, but maybe it's a fact. It's possible that you simply didn't fit what the editors were looking for. This is why it's important to read the magazine, journal or blog before you submit. Other editors will take a minute to send you criticism or commentary. Savor this. The editor is telling you what might get you in the next time.

You can submit to magazine that actually prints paper copies or you can submit to online journals. You can also enter contests. Many contests offer finalists publication in the journal, some offer prize money to winners. There are also grants available for writers from state and regional governments, universities and foundations. A good source of information on these is the Poets and Writers website.

As you're trying to sell your work, there are a few personalities you'll need to navigate, too. Let's start with an agent, your agent. This is the person who will help you get your work ready to publish and who will present it to the publisher. He or she represents you, for a fee, usually 10 to 15 percent of your book's sale price. This is how he or she pays bills, so it is in their interest to sell your book. The agent should not charge you to do the work. Fee-for-service agents are probably not a good deal.

There are relatively standard contracts and there are organizations that will go over your agent's contract to make sure you're getting a fair deal. It's probably worth joining a group that will do this for you at least the first time. A good place to start is with the Association of Author's Representatives or a service like Writer's Market or Writer's Digest.

Interview potential agents. Always ask about recent sales. Has this person sold books like yours before or does he specialize in books about unicorns. Make sure you and this person communicate well together. Your agent needs to "get you," to understand who you are and what you're about. This person is your representative and is carrying your work forward. Make sure he or she really knows you. This probably requires a face-to-face meeting.

What can you expect? Your agent will read your work and make suggestions for revisions. Yes, your work will likely need more revision. Your agent will help you construct a book proposal and take that to publishers to try to sell it. If it sells the agent does the negotiating to get the best deal for you (and her since she gets a percentage). He will seek to sell the work for additional rights—movies or foreign sales for example. The agent will also go over the contract with the publisher and track payments to your account on the part of the publisher.

A final note on agents: these are the people whose appreciation of the value of writing is go great that they do many, many things they don't want to do to help people like us get published. They are in the business for many of the same reasons you are: because they love the art.

The publisher is the person who takes your book, prints it, sends it out to bookstores and advertises it. Publishers come in many different forms. Big publishers like Simon and Schuster, Penguin, Harper Collins, Knopf and others operate primarily out of New York City. They represent the glamorous end of the business—big money, big advertisement, big sales. Smaller publishers exist pretty much everywhere. I've worked with publishers in Baltimore, Tucson and Winston-Salem. These publishers generally don't generate big money or big advertising. But they get your book out into the world where you can run with it.

If you don't have an agent, you'll have to try to sell your book to publishers yourself. Look at websites or publications by Writers Digest, Writers Market, and Poets & Writers. Also, go to conventions and book fairs to meet small publishers. Think of it like speed dating.

Some publishers will offer to publish your book for a fee. These are called subsidy presses. The author pays the publisher for a series of services: editing, printing and marketing the book. For writers whose wish is simply to put their work in front of others and for whom the work of finding an agent, selling the book to a publisher, going through the work of editing and then marketing the book seems too much, this is a perfectly acceptable route to publication. But *caveat emptor*, use the same techniques to vet a subsidy publisher you would in choosing an agent.

Self-publishing is a burgeoning market where the author skips the agent and publisher route and puts the work out in the public on his own. This can be in paper form, or electronically, or both. The things to keep in mind here are that no one else is serving as the gatekeeper for you. It is probably worth hiring a freelance editor to help you get the book ready. Your publishing house will take care of typesetting and printing. These types of books were, until recently, unlikely to earn a profit for the author. But because of internet publishing and print on demand, a select few authors have recently done quite well. There was a *New York Times* Magazine article in 2011 about a writer who sold 9,000 e-books a day.

For shorter works there are journals and magazines. The expansion of these thanks to the internet has been Malthusian. There are thousands of legitimate online journals now added to the long list of paper journals in which writers can place their works whether as essays, short stories, flash fiction, or poetry.

All good libraries and bookstores have shelves of literary journals and magazines in their periodicals sections. Poets & Writers, Writer's Market, Writer's Digest and Duotrope all have extensive lists of journals. Some advice: Read the journal before submitting. Make certain you are a good fit for the magazine before you spend your time submitting. Make a list of ten or twenty journals or magazines you would like to see your work in.

Once you have the list, create a submission matrix that lists the top three, the second tier of three and so on. Submit to the first three magazines simultaneously. Many journals require that you use Submittable or Duotrope to submit your work to them, so it's probably worth getting your profile set up and opening an account (free for the moment) now. Both also offer an onsite submissions tracker. But I think it's still worth keeping your own matrix.

Some journals are adamant that they do not accept simultaneous submissions. So what? If you get are lucky enough to get picked up by two magazines simultaneously, pick the best of the two and plead a gracious ignorance of the policy with the second. In the event your work isn't selected by the first tier journals or magazines you submit to, submit to the second tier, and so on until you find your niche.

We talked a bit earlier about contests. They are another way to get your work noticed. Here again, you are paying to get your work noticed or even read, so some people shy away from these as they might from a subsidy press. However, the value to entering contests is that you might actually win. Winning usually guarantees publication and additional notice, it adds a line to your writer's resume, and it sometimes comes with prize money or some other perquisite.

So that's it. We're really done this time. You're ready to go. Regardless of your objectives—to publish, to provide a story for your family, or simply to get your story told and gain control of it—now you should be better prepared. So take a walk and clear your mind, then come back and start writing.

Keep writing.

Appendix A
Veteran Writers featured in this book.

Amis, Kingsley (1922-1995) Novelist, poet, critic. Served in the Royal Signals Corps during World War II

Babel, Isaac (1984-1940) Journalist, novelist, short story writer. Babel served on the Romanian Front during the Russian Revolution in 1917. He later rode with the Red Cavalry, primarily as a journalist.

Bierce, Ambrose (1842-1913) Journalist, short story writer. Bierce served in the Union Army during the Civil War. He saw significant combat including Shiloh and Kennesaw Mountain.

Brittain, Vera (1893-1970) Poet, memoirist. Brittain served as a field nurse in the First World War.

Calvino, Italo (1923-1985) Novelist and journalist. Avoided being drafted in the Italian fascist army in WWII, Calvino fought against the Nazis in the Garibaldi Brigades in 1944 and 1945.

Caputo, Philip (1941-   ) Novelist, journalist. Caputo served as a Marine infantry officer in the Vietnam.

Cheever, John (1912-1982) Novelist and short story writer. Cheever served in the Infantry and later the Signal Corps during World War II.

Crane, Stephen (1871-1900) Journalist, novelist. Crane was a cadet but never joined the regular army. However during the Spanish American War when he was working as a correspondent he volunteered and was commended for service as a courier, the dangerous job of carrying messages between commanders under fire.

Defoe, Daniel (1661-1731) Novelist. Although never a professional soldier, Defoe fought alongside the Duke of Monmouth in the Monmouth Rebellion against King James II.

Faulkner, William (1897-1962) Novelist. Winner of the Nobel Prize for Literature. Too short for the American Army, Faulkner enlisted in the British Royal Flying Corps during WWI.

Fleming, Ian (1908-1964) Novelist, journalist. Fleming was a soldier in the Black Watch but is much better known as a Naval Intelligence officer—his code number was 17F. He commanded 30 Commando and T-Force during the Second World War.

Ford, Ford Madox (1873-1939) Novelist and poet. Ford, born Ford Hermann Heuffner, served in France with the Welch Regiment in the First World War.

Forsyth, Frederick (1938-   ) Novelist. One of the youngest pilots ever to serve in the Royal Air Force.

Fowles, John (1926-2005) Novelist. Served in the Royal Marines just at the end of the Second World War.

Golding, William (1911-1993) Novelist, poet and playwright. Awarded the Nobel Prize for Literature. Served in the Royal Navy during World War II including command of a landing ship at D-Day.

Heller, Joseph (1923-1999) Novelist, short story writer, playwright. Heller served as bombardier in a B25 during World War II. He flew on 60 combat missions in Europe.

Hemingway, Ernest. (1899-1961) Novelist, journalist, short-story writer. Winner of the Nobel Prize for Literature. Served as an ambulance driver in World War One.

Holmes, Oliver Wendell (1841-1935) Jurist, historian. Holmes served in the Union Army as an infantry officer in numerous battles including the Peninsula Campaign and the Wilderness.

Kennedy, Kelly. (1970-   ) Journalist. Kennedy served in the Army taking part in the Gulf War and Operation Restore Hope in Somalia. She was an embedded journalist with an Army infantry company in Iraq.

Lawrence, T.E. (Thomas Edward) (1888-1935) Memoirist. Awarded the Distinguished Service Order after organizing the Arab revolt in the western desert during World War One. Lawrence also served as a non-rated (enlisted) airman.

Manning, Frederic (1882-1935) Memoirist, novelist. Manning served as an enlisted soldier and later, an officer in the British Army during World War One.

Mason, A.E.W. (1865-1948) Novelist. Served as a soldier and Royal Marine during the First World War.

McKenna, Richard (1913-1954) Novelist. Mckenna was a career sailor serving over 20 years in World War II and Korea. He retired as a Chief Machinist Mate and used his GI Bill benefits to attend college.

Maugham, Somerset (1874-1965) Novelist, playwright, short story writer. Ambulance driver in World War I (along with John Dos Passos and E.E. Cummings).

de Maupassant, Guy (1850-1892) Novelist. Soldier in the Franco-Prussian war.

Michener, James (1907-1997) Novelist. Michener served in the U.S. Navy in the Pacific theater during the Second World War.

Morgan, Ted (Sanche de Gramont) (1932-   ) Biographer, memoirist. Morgan served in the French Army in Algeria in 1956.

O'Brien, Tim (1946-   ) Novelist. O'Brien served in the infantry in Vietnam

Owen, Wilfred (1893-1918) Poet. Owen was a British infantry officer in the First World War. He was awarded the Military Cross.

Perec, Georges (1936-1982) Novelist. Perec served in the 18th Parachute Regiment in the French Army.

Roth, Joseph (1894-1939) Journalist and novelist. Served in the Imperial Habsburg Army during World War I.

Salinger, J.D. (1919-2010) Novelist and short story writer. Served in the U.S. Army during WWII. Went ashore on D-Day with the 4th Infantry Division. Fought through the Huertgen Forest and the Battle of the Bulge.

Sassoon, Siegfried (1816-1967) Poet and memoirist. Infantry officer with the British Army during the First World War. Awarded the Military Cross for gallantry.

Stendhal (Marie-Henri Beyle) (1783-1842) Novelist. Served as a soldier in Napolean's 1812 invasion of Russia.

Tolkien, John Ronald Ruell (J.R.R.) (1892-1973) Novelist. Served as a signal officer in the British Army at the Somme in World War One.

Tolstoy, Leo (1828-1910) Novelist. Soldier in the Crimean War.

Vonnegut, Kurt (1922-2007) Novelist. An enlisted soldier in the 106th Infantry Division, Vonnegut was captured by the Nazis at the Battle of the Bulge. Imprisoned in Dresden, he survived the firebombing of Dresden by the U.S. Army Air Forces.

Webb, James (1946-   ) Novelist. Webb served as a Marine officer in Vietnam. Awarded the Navy Cross and Silver Star Medal, he was later Secretary of the Navy and a U.S. Senator.

Wolff, Tobias (1945-   ) Novelist, short story writer, memoirist. Special Forces officer in Vietnam.

Wouk, Herman (1915-   ) Novelist. Winner of the Pulitzer Prize. A naval officer, he served on destroyers during World War II.

Appendix B
A Reading List

This list is not intended to be all inclusive. It is a good jumping off point for what should be a lifetime of reading for you. All of these authors and poets are veterans or the family members of veterans.

Kingsley Amis: *Lucky Jim* and others.
Nelson Algren: *The Man with the Golden Arm*.
Ambrose Bierce: Any collection of this stories.
Isaac Babel: *The Red Cavalry Stories.*
Vera Brittain: *The Testament of Youth.*
Rupert Brooke: any collection of his poems.
Shannon Cain (ed): *Powder: Writing by Women in the Ranks.*
Philip Caputo: *A Rumor of War.*
John Cheever: Any collection of his stories.
Stephen Crane: *The Red Badge of Courage.*
E.E. Cummings: Any collection of his poems.
James Dickey, poetry and novels.
Andre Dubus, any collection of his short stories.
Siobhan Fallon: *You Know When the Men are Gone.*
Ford Madox Ford: *The Good Soldier, No More Parades, others.*
Frederic Forsyth: *Day of the Jackal, The Dogs of War.*
John Fowles: *The French Lieutenant's Woman, The Magus.*
George MacDonald Fraser: *Quartered Safe out Here* or any of his *Flashman* books.
William Faulkner: Any of his novels.
William Golding: *Lord of the Flies.*
Gunter Grass: *The Tin Drum.*
Robert Graves, *Goodbye to All That.*
Joseph Heller: *Catch-22.*
Anthony Hecht: Any of his books of poetry.
Ernest Hemingway: *For Whom the Bell Tolls*; *A Farewell to Arms*, and many, many others.
James Jones: *From Here to Eternity, The Thin Red Line, Whistle.*

Kelly Kennedy: *They Fought for Each Other.*
Yusuf Komunyakaa: Any collection of his poems.
Ellen LaMotte: *The Backwash of War*
T.E. Lawrence: *The Seven Pillars of Wisdom.*
Christopher Logue: *All Day Permanent Red, War Music, Cold Calls.*
Anthony Loyd: *My War Gone By: I Miss It So.*
Frederic Manning: *Her Privates We.*
James Mathews: *Last Known Position.*
Somerset Maugham: *Moon and Sixpence, Of Human Bondage.*
Guy de Maupassant: Any collection of his stories.
Richard McKenna: *The Sand Pebbles.*
Tim O'Brien: *The Things They Carried, In the Lake of the Woods.*
Wilfred Owen: any collection of his poems.
Erich Maria Remarque: *All Quiet on the Western Front, The Road Home* and others.
Joseph Roth: *The Radetzky March.*
Isaac Rosenberg: any collection of his poems.
J.D. Salinger: *Nine Stories* and his novels.
James Salter: *The Hunters* and any of his many other books.
Siegfried Sassoon: any collection of his poems.
Charles Simic: Any collection of his poems, and *The Renegade.*
Stendahl: *The Charterhouse of Parma.*
Jeff Stein: *A Murder in Wartime.*
Anthony Swofford: *Jarhead.*
Gay Talese: *Thy Neighbor's Wife*, "Frank Sinatra Has A Cold," "Mr. Bad News," many other books and articles.
Leo Tolstoy: *War and Peace, Anna Karenina.*
Brian Turner: *Here, Bullet.*
Kurt Vonnegut: *Slaughterhouse Five* and many others.
Evelyn Waugh: *The Sword of Honor Trilogy, many others.*
Jim Webb: *Fields of Fire.*
Richard Wilbur: Any collection of his poems, *Deliverance.*
Kayla Williams: *Love My Rifle More Then You*
Tobias Wolff: *In Pharaoh's Army; In the World* (short stories).
Herman Wouk: *The Caine Mutiny.*

ABOUT THE AUTHOR

Ron Capps served in the U.S. Army, Army Reserve, and National Guard for a combined 25 years. He is a combat veteran of Afghanistan, served on peacekeeping duty in the Darfur region of Sudan and in Chad, and took part in a Non-Combatant Evacuation during a military mutiny in the Central African Republic. His duty assignments included service in the 111th Field Artillery, 11th Armored Cavalry Regiment, 2nd Infantry Division, XVIII Airborne Corps, Special Operations Command-Europe, U.S. Army Operations Group, U.S. Army Foreign Intelligence Command, and the Defense Intelligence Agency.

Ron is the author of *Seriously Not All Right: Five Wars in Ten Years*, a memoir published by Schaffner Press. He is a graduate of the Master of Liberal Arts and a distinguished graduate of the MA in Writing programs of the Johns Hopkins University with a dual concentration in fiction and non-fiction writing. His policy writing and commentary have appeared in Time Magazine and Foreign Policy, in The American Interest, Health Affairs, Monday Developments, on Pacifica Radio, the BBC World Service and NPR's *All Things Considered*. He has been a consultant or subject matter expert for Rolling Stone, Vanity Fair, PBS *Frontline* and *The Newshour*. His literary writing has appeared in the literary journal JMWW, Prime Number magazine, the Little Patuxent Review, The New York Times, The Delmarva Review, and Riverlit; it has been anthologized by Press 53 and milspeak.com, and listed in the Best American Essays series. He is represented by the John W. Wright literary agency.

Ron founded the Veterans Writing Program in 2011.

THE VETERANS WRITING PROJECT

The Veterans Writing Project is a 501(c)(3) non-profit based in Washington, DC. Founded in 2011, the VWP provides no-cost writing seminars and workshops for veterans, active and reserve service members, and military family members.

VWP seminars are led by working writers who have MA or MFA writing degrees and who are also combat veterans.

Writing War: A Guide to Telling Your Own Story is our curriculum

The VWP also publishes the journal *O-Dark-Thirty.*

www.veteranswriting.org

www.o-dark-thirty.org

The Veterans Writing Project
6508 Barnaby St NW
Washington DC 20015

Made in the USA
Middletown, DE
22 September 2015